WESTCOASTERS

WESTCOASTERS

BOATS THAT BUILT BRITISH COLUMBIA

TOM HENRY

HARBOUR PUBLISHING

Published by
HARBOUR PUBLISHING
P.O. Box 219
Madeira Park, BC Canada
V0N 2H0

Cover painting of the tug *Lorne* and square rigger off the mouth of Juan de Fuca Strait by Robert McVittie
Design and page composition by Martin Nichols, Lionheart Graphics
Editing by Andrew Scott
Printed and bound in Canada by Friesen Printers

Harbour Publishing acknowledges the financial support of the Government of Canada through the Book Publishing Industry Development Program and the Province of British Columbia through the British Columbia Arts Council, for its publishing activities.

Canadian Cataloguing in Publication Data

Henry, Tom, 1961–
    Westcoasters

    ISBN 1-55017-190-9

    1. Boats and boating—British Columbia—History. 2. Ships—British Columbia—History. I. Title.

VK27.B7H46 1998   387.2'09711   C98-910674-8

THE CANADA COUNCIL | LE CONSEIL DES ARTS
FOR THE ARTS | DU CANADA
SINCE 1957 | DEPUIS 1957

Contents

Preface

On the morning of Thursday, December 16, 1791, an officer of the Royal Navy stepped from a horse-drawn carriage onto the wharves at Deptford, on the south bank of the River Thames. Deptford was home to the Victualling Board, the provisioning centre for the navy's great voyages, and as the officer strode along the docks, he noted the coiled hawsers, fine spars, and barrels of sauerkraut and salt pork. The air carried its own inventory too: sweet tars and bitter oakum and the must of wet canvas. Though there were many fine vessels at the dock, the officer did not pause until he was alongside an inglorious three-masted ship. One hundred feet long, barge-like in its dimensions, it was the type of craft that is generously described as sturdy. The officer, a pudgy man with a religious bearing and grey, yellow-flecked eyes, appraised the ship for a moment, then, without ceremony, marched up the gangplank.

I say this is where BC history begins. Not West Coast history, for that is rooted in the tidal shifts of glaciers; nor is it Native history, traceable, depending on your belief, to the existence of a land bridge linking Asia to Alaska 12,000 years ago, or to a raven's playfulness. No; it is the seed of BC—that writhing, ill-named burgoo of Natives, non-Natives, logged-off valleys, timbered cities, beautiful, stinky pulp mills, seaweed poets, freaky politicians and big mountains that Jack Hodgins called "the Ragged Green Edge of the World."

And it begins on a creaky gangplank two hundred years ago.

The man was Captain George Vancouver. The ship was the *Discovery*. The two were about to set off from England on a journey of exploration to the northwest coast of North America that would last four and a half years. The trip changed the region forever. Prior to the *Discovery*'s journey, the coast was a Native domain; to Europeans, it was a mystery, a blank on the globe where armchair geographers doodled ancient fancies, such as the passage to China. The *Discovery* slaughtered the dream and replaced it with a map. With Vancouver's intricate charts in hand, European empire builders could draw lines through the land, rename, reallocate, give and take—all the things that define a country, as opposed to a land. Awkward and resilient, the *Discovery* marked both the end of Native dominance of the Northwest, and the ascendance of European-style notions of geography, property and politics.

Nor was the *Discovery* the only important ship in BC history. It was succeeded by the *Beaver*, a black and dirty little steamer that played so many roles in nineteenth-century coastal history that it is best understood as a fleet rather than an individual ship. The *Beaver* was followed by the *William Irving*, a Fraser River sternwheeler as grand as the family that ran it; the Dunsmuirs' trend-setting tug *Lorne*; the glorious Victoria-based clipper *Thermopylae*; and the humble, seemingly indestructible ship-of-all-trades, the *Beatrice*. The first three decades of the twentieth century are synonymous with some amazing ships, too, including the "Bible barge" *Columbia*, the Canadian Pacific Railway's adored *Princess Maquinna*, pioneer rumrunner-cum-log carrier the *Malahat*, and the Union Steamships' premier "Daddy boat," the fine *Lady Alexandra*. No account of modern BC could omit the deep-sea salvage tug *Sudbury*, the less glamorous but equally important classic wooden-hulled seiner the *BCP No. 45*, or the *Pisces*, an improbable 1960s-era submersible that fixed Vancouver at the centre of the underwater high-technology world. And finally, the book closes with a chapter on Bill Reid's quest-inspired dugout *Lootaas*, whose magnificent hull is a powerful symbol in the long, often-troubled, often-heroic rise of Native culture from the deprivations instigated by European newcomers in the era of the *Discovery*.

Fourteen boats, in some ways as subjective as my choice of shirts. But I'll trust the list to stand on a simple explanation: while it would be as easy as falling off a yardarm to *add* a dozen worthy ships to this account, you'd be bucking the current to argue any of the mentioned boats *out*. Each of these vessels helped define the coast, gave it some of the shape, character, sound, humanity that distinguish it today. Take away just one and the story springs a plank, takes on water, founders. From sloop to canoe, the careers of these ships overlap, like the planks on a lapstrake hull, so it is possible to read the province's history through their stories. Call them west coasters; they are ships that built BC.

Discovery

For a nation with great maritime pretensions, Britain in the late 1700s built some awful ships. Stubby in the bow and stern, they looked extruded instead of crafted. One contemporary accused shipyards of "building ships by the mile and cutting them off to length as required." They had the sailing qualities of a scow, but not the stability. Many capsized. The most famous example was the *Royal George*, which heeled and sank while lying off Spithead in 1782, with a loss of nine hundred lives.

By the time the *Discovery* was built, in 1789, the worst features of British naval architecture had been eradicated. If the hulls were still not swift, they were at least seaworthy. Their greatest virtue was strength: the *Discovery*'s melon-shaped merchant hull was built from heavy oak timbers, assembled around a massive keel of elm. The Royal Navy added ten 4-pound cannons, installed accommodation for one hundred and called it a sloop-of-war. It was, in effect, an armed bus. Though stout, it was slow and cumbersome, traits that had direct bearing on the nature of Vancouver's work in the confined waters of the Northwest Coast.

CAPTAIN GEORGE VANCOUVER'S SLOOP-OF-WAR *DISCOVERY*, FOLLOWED BY THE ARMED TENDER *CHATHAM*. *DISCOVERY* IS A FAMOUS NAME IN THE HISTORY OF EXPLORATION. THE FIRST *DISCOVERY* EXPLORED HUDSON STRAIT IN 1604, AND THE LEGENDARY NAVIGATOR CAPT. JAMES COOK TOOK ANOTHER ON HIS THIRD AND LAST VOYAGE. VANCOUVER'S *DISCOVERY* WAS A CONVERTED COLLIER-STYLE SHIP, A COMMON TYPE OF CRAFT KNOWN FOR STRENGTH OF CONSTRUCTION.

The *Discovery* also had quirks that affected the ensuing voyage. George Vancouver noticed one the day he joined the ship. The yard on the main mast was too short. The yard, or spar, worked as a derrick to launch the heavy ship's boats from the decks. To use the boats, Vancouver would have to replace the yard with another long enough to reach beyond the side of the hull. Vancouver was similarly distressed with a glass greenhouse on the *Discovery*'s afterdeck, a vulnerable-looking structure meant to house collected plants destined for the Royal Gardens at Kew. It was just the kind of ill-conceived, experimental add-on that had always been foisted on exploration vessels, and Vancouver rightly saw it as a hazard. (The glass house nurtured a foul mood in Vancouver that lasted the entire voyage.) Artists on the voyage found the structure so ugly and unnautical that they left it out of their sketches.

The botch-up with the spars was typical of the *Discovery*'s departure, or, rather, intended departure. The ship was originally scheduled to leave for the Northwest Coast in 1790. When relations between Spain and England—both with deep interests in the northwest—imploded, the Admiralty held off dispatching the modestly armed *Discovery*. While waiting for the situation to mend, the voyage's intended leader, Captain Henry Roberts, was assigned to the West Indies, and George Vancouver was assigned command of the ship. He was thirty-two years old.

Born in the busy port town of King's Lynn, Norfolk, Vancouver went to sea as a midshipman with the great British navigator, Captain James Cook. Cook, who joined the Royal Navy as an able-bodied seaman, believed good officers, like good ships, were founded on sound keels. First came sails, then the sextant. He started Vancouver aloft, scrambling among the web of slings and jeers and leechlines. Labouring far above the deck, his gut jackknifed around a spar, Vancouver learned what it was like to reef the main topgallant sail in a blow, or wrest with a tangled clew line. When he had mastered the practical side of sailing, Vancouver schooled at Cook's shoulder in the arts of observation, ship maintenance, hydrographic surveying and navigation. Each task, Cook drilled, had to be performed with precision; upon them rested the success and survival of the ship and crew.

For all his study, however, Vancouver was never Cook's equal as a leader. He

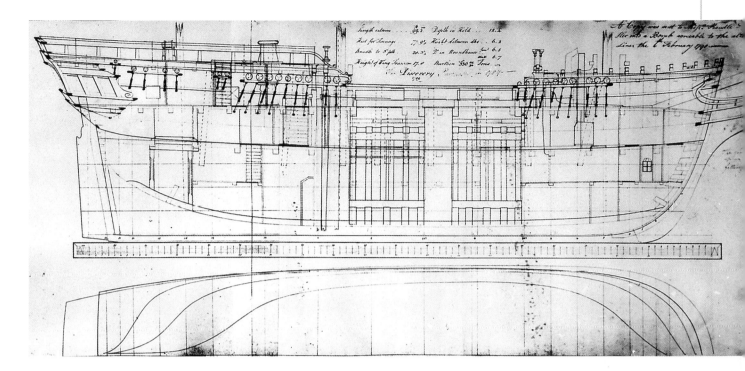

lacked the intangible but crucial art of getting along. Whether a result of Vancouver's cushy childhood (he got a position with Cook partly because of a family connection with the Earl of Sandwich, the First Lord of the Admiralty) or ill health (he may have suffered from myxedema, a thyroid deficiency), he was often surly and miserable. This reputation trudged ahead of him from Cook's ship, through his years with Lord Rodney's fleet in the West Indies, and onto the docks at Deptford.

While the ship prepared to sail, many of the crew, hand picked by Captain Roberts, signed up elsewhere or "ran," as desertion was called. According to George Goodman Hewitt, a surgeon's mate on the *Discovery*, this was a direct result of "Vans. Character for Passion & Tyranny [which] was well known among the good Seamen of the Navy." Before leaving England the *Discovery* lost sixteen men, including Richard Richards, a boatswain who embarrassingly absconded with ship's supplies.

The result was that the *Discovery* sailed with a less-than-ideal crew. "[N]otwithstanding the Admiralty orders that none but able Seamen should be taken in her," wrote Hewitt, the ship "was obliged to be sent out with a ragged Complement of Fishermans Boys and other Fresh water Sailors." Many of the replacements arrived via the press gangs. These "reluctant voyagers," as historian Robin Fisher calls them, would cause much woe on the voyage.

It should be noted that Hewitt was a relentless critic of Vancouver. His copy of Vancouver's published account of the journey is awash in scrawls and notes, all derisive. But even Vancouver's admirers admitted he was prone to sudden and inexplicable outbursts of temper. One of these supporters, Robert Barrie, a nineteen-year-old midshipman, joined the ship during final preparations. A letter he wrote to his mother reflects his nervous estimation: "Cpt Vancouver is in my opinion a verry good fellow but verry passionate."

THE *DISCOVERY*'S HEAVILY BUILT HULL SURVIVED THE GROUNDINGS THAT OCCUR INEVITABLY DURING VOYAGES INTO UNCHARTED WATERS. ONE HISTORIAN SPECULATES THAT THE *DISCOVERY*'S UNUSUAL RAKING STEM AND FLARED BOW SUGGEST EARLY USE OF TANK TESTING IN SHIP DESIGN.

Vancouver first sailed the *Discovery* during a short hop from the Thames to Falmouth, near Land's End. En route, the ship hit a storm in the English Channel. The storm was severe, but nothing more than might be expected in a trans-oceanic voyage. Even so, heavy seas swept away the ship's head, including the "seats of ease," as toilets were called. Also carried off were the bumpkins, or spars extending forward from the head. This loss was more serious. To the end of the bumpkins was attached the weather clew of the foresail, which enabled the ship to manoeuvre. Without the bumpkins, the *Discovery*'s ability to change course was shackled. After several extremely tense hours, the storm abated and the *Discovery* made its way to Falmouth for final provisioning and, yet again, more repairs.

Finally, on April 1, 1791, the *Discovery* and the armed tender *Chatham* set sail from England. The crew joked about the omens implicit in departing on All Fool's Day, but Vancouver did not share their levity. If his mood was to be summarized in a word, that word would be vile. He had problems with the ship. Many of his best crew had left. He was behind schedule. The only good thing to say as he watched the green paddocks of the Cornwall coast slump into the horizon was that they were finally under way. But Vancouver's problems were not over. As he soon realized, the *Discovery* was not a fast-travelling ship, a fact largely lost on historians because, compared with the wretched *Chatham*, the *Discovery* seemed swift and nimble. Early in the voyage there was some question as to whether the *Chatham* would stay afloat. After one terrible session, when the *Chatham* nearly capsized, the ship had to be reballasted with 662 rounds of the *Discovery*'s 4-pound shot. Then Vancouver decided to set into Santa Cruz, in the Canary Islands, where the *Chatham* took on 23 tons of shale. The stop created its own troubles. While at Santa Cruz some sailors off the *Discovery* got drunk and started a fight. Vancouver and several officers, ashore at the time, attempted the break up the fracas. One officer was beaten on the head, another nearly impaled on a bayonet, and Vancouver was picked up and thrown into the scum-laden harbour.

In the open ocean again, the *Chatham*, which Vancouver diplomatically called a "crank" and its own crew called "our Dung-Barge," proved a perturbing sailer. The *Discovery*'s log is littered with references to the *Chatham*'s poor sailing. Yet, the *Discovery* seems to have managed little better. At one point in the Atlantic, on the way to the Cape of Good Hope, Vancouver signalled the *Chatham* that he was going to surge ahead. They would rendezvous in port. After four days of hard sailing, however, the *Chatham*'s stubby little sails could still be seen over the *Discovery*'s stern. When the *Discovery* finally arrived at the Cape, it found the *Chatham* bobbing at anchor, having arrived a full day earlier. The little craft was to confound its own crew, and Vancouver, with occasional prodigious bursts of speed.

At sea, far from the influence of English mores and Admiralty orders, the *Discovery* became a strange dominion. Vancouver was lord; the ship's structure the geography. For months at a time it received no word from the outside world. Even along the

Northwest Coast, enfolded by mountains, surrounded by strange people, it remained insular. It had a culture, crime, a class system. It even had its own agrarian economy. At various times on the voyage, the ship's decks were home to pigs, goats, chicken, cattle, sheep and, inexplicably, a Newfoundland dog. The ship smelled and sounded like a barn. Vancouver's idea was to slaughter some of the farm animals at sea for fresh meat, and drop others off on Pacific islands to start stocks. The sheep, housed on deck in the open ship's boats, did not travel well; only two of thirty taken on board at Portsmouth made it to the table. The rest died and were heaved overboard.

The *Discovery*'s human cargo was no less eclectic. The ship carried a complement of eighty-six, plus fourteen marines. All but one were bachelors. Among the non-essential crew was a twenty-year-old Hawaiian named Towereroo. Towereroo was listed in the ships' companies as John Ingram, but preferred to be called Jack. He had left Molokai at age eleven or twelve on the *Princess Royal*. In China he transferred to the *Princess of Wales* and arrived in England in 1789. He was sent to private school but, according to Vancouver, all he learned was how to draw "rude pictures." After a trip to Hudson Bay he returned to England, where he joined *Discovery* for the return journey to his homeland.

Towereroo wanted off the *Discovery*. Several troublesome characters on board had to be ordered off, in fact. The most notorious of these was the Honorable Thomas Pitt, relative of William Pitt, the British prime minister. A whiner and sniveller, the younger Pitt had signed on as midshipman, a gentleman-in-training, just as Vancouver had on Cook's ship. He was a worse-than-useless addition to the expedition, often quarrelling with other officers. Several times Vancouver had him lashed for insolence, and once he was chained to the mast. Vancouver eventually gave up trying to transform the aristocrat into a seaman and sent Pitt home in the supply ship *Daedalus*. Disgraced, Pitt never forgave Vancouver for what he thought was gross mistreatment.

At least some of the crew troubles on the *Discovery* (and there were many) are attributable to overcrowding. One hundred men aboard a 100-foot-long ship, packed with animals and supplies, left no room for privacy. Nor was such a large crew needed to run the ship. But the Royal Navy insisted on the complement because it fully expected many crew members to perish during the voyage, especially of scurvy,

DESPITE THE VICIOUS MURDER OF CAPTAIN COOK IN FEBRUARY 1779 AT KEALAKEKUA BAY IN HAWAII, THE ISLAND CONTINUED TO BE AN IMPORTANT WINTERING PORT BETWEEN THE *DISCOVERY*'S SUMMER EXPLORATIONS OF THE NORTHWEST COAST.

the bane of long maritime expeditions. The trouble was, few died. (Six altogether, none of scurvy.) Thanks to Vancouver's insistence on regular rations of spruce beer, greens and "rob" (distilled juice) of lemon, the crew were remarkably healthy.

Overcrowding led to anger, outbursts and frustration. In the forecastle, especially, where the seamen and marines slept, the conditions were horrific. Hammocks, slung from ceilings less than 6 feet high, billowed from every beam. There was little natural light, and the oil lanterns gave off a feeble, sallow glow. The quarters were cold. They stunk. The mainstay stenches of sweat, moldy clothing and rotten teeth were displaced only by the acrid reek of smoke, blasted from a downdraft through the woodstove. The men bickered, fought, became listless. Joseph Murgatroyd, a forty-year-old carpenter's mate, apparently suffering from depression, steadied himself on the bulwarks, then dove silently into the sea. He was never seen again.

The *Discovery* made landfall on the shore of North America at Cabrillo Point, California, in mid-April of 1792. The ship turned north and sailed along the coast, keeping land in sight during the day, then hauled off and tacked during the night. Along the coast of what is now Oregon, the crew noticed a silt-grey plume of water emerging from the landward side. Such colour often indicated a river. They scanned the shore but could see only breakers. With the memory of the *Discovery*'s troubles in the English Channel storm still fresh in his mind, Vancouver wisely decided against taking his ship closer. Thus he famously missed the Columbia River. It was an oversight for which he suffered much historical cavilling, though, rightly, blame (or credit) should be seen as an inevitable result of the *Discovery*'s sailing limitations. The later charting and naming of the river, by Captain Robert Gray, an American, was a key card in US claims to the area.

Soon after arriving in the Juan de Fuca Strait, Vancouver realized the *Discovery* and the *Chatham* were too awkward for surveying the intricate waterways and shoreline. Instead, he decided to send crew out in the ship's boats—small, sail- and oar-powered craft carried on the decks of the *Discovery* and lowered on the yards. They radiated out from the larger ships into the nearby waters, exploring the inlets and islands. As the crew rowed they took compass bearings of prominent features of the land and meticulous measurements of the course of the boat. To this information were added sextant observations recorded during frequent trips ashore, which gave the direction of the land and tangents to islands. Back on board the *Discovery*, the data was transferred to a plotting sheet. As each area was charted, the ships would let go the anchor and move on. These surveys went along for three years; each summer the *Discovery* and the *Chatham* worked on the coast, then retreated to Hawaii during the winter.

Though this method of surveying was accurate, it was also slow and difficult. One crew rowed over 600 nautical miles in twenty-three days; their efforts forwarded the survey of the coastline by a mere 52 nautical miles. Assigned to one of the ship's boats, a crew would set out from the *Discovery* and row or sail into the myriad inlets

and passageways along the coast. They didn't know where they were going or who they would meet. Though provisioned with hardtack and grog, they often lived off the land. They ate crab, duck, beaver, goose, goosander, bear cub, seal and seal pup, "curlews" (probably sandpipers) and "March Sampire" (likely *Salicornia virginica*, or glasswort). A mainstay was crows. Once, they shot an old black bear, but although they "were living on salted provisions, its flesh did not seem much relished." When they could, they traded with Native people for "bread of pine bark," a dried mix of pulped spruce bark, berries, salmon and herring eggs. Only once did their eclectic eating habits lead to trouble. That was when John Carter, a twenty-four-year-old seaman, died of paralytic shellfish poisoning, after eating mussels in Finlayson Channel in June 1793.

Away from the *Discovery*, the crews in the little boats had more frequent contact with the Native people of the coast. With one exception, relations were serviceable, if not good. They traded knives and coppers for food and novelties. Though Vancouver was not especially interested in aboriginal culture, some of his officers were. They were intrigued with the flocks of "wool dogs" whose fleece the Natives mixed with duck down and the cotton of fireweed to make blankets. At Friendly Cove,

ONE OF THE *DISCOVERY*'S SHIP'S BOATS CHARTS BURRARD INLET IN 1792. THE TWIN MOUNTAIN PEAKS KNOWN AS THE LIONS RISE IN THE BACKGROUND.

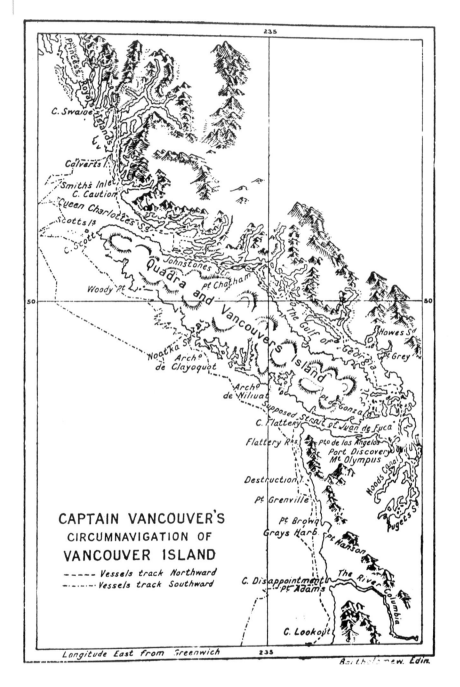

CAPTAIN VANCOUVER'S
CIRCUMNAVIGATION OF
VANCOUVER ISLAND

----- *Vessels track Northward*
-·-·-·- *Vessels track Southward*

Longitude East from Greenwich

Bartholomew. Edin.

VANCOUVER WAS THE FIRST
EUROPEAN TO CIRCUMNAVI-
GATE VANCOUVER ISLAND.

on the west coast of Vancouver Island, British sailors were particularly fascinated with a captured hummingbird. The bird was leashed with a long human hair tied to a leg. One sailor wanted the bird so badly he made its owner a good offer. A deal was struck. Other Natives, recognizing a promising market, disappeared into the woods. Several hours later they returned, every man, woman and child with three or four hummingbirds. The abundance overstocked the market, and within minutes sailors were getting two birds for a single brass button.

The story about the hummingbirds speaks, however anecdotally, to a more serious matter of relations between aboriginal people and whites at the time. Contrary to some readings of history, which declare gullible Natives were inevitably exploited by crafty Europeans, the journals from the *Discovery* and other explorers suggest that, at a very minimum, relations were equal and, at times, often favoured Natives. Native people, who had food and furs in abundance, needed iron, blankets and guns. Explorers, who had blankets and iron, needed food and information. The relative value of the goods fluctuated with supply and demand, just as it would in the most sophisticated London exchanges. It wasn't until much later, when aboriginals became incidental to white affairs, that they were marginalized. (If anything, Native power was in ascendance in the mid-1790s. According to Vancouver, the aboriginals were "daily becoming formidable." He thought it highly likely that a systematic survey would have been impossible had the *Discovery* arrived even a year later.)

There was a certain cultural reciprocity, too, based on a natural misunderstanding of foreign culture. If European traders thought the Natives primitive, the

Natives had the same notions about Europeans. They were particularly intrigued by some of the very habits that Europeans thought civilized, like carrying a handkerchief. To Natives, who blew their noses onto the ground, the European habit of blowing the nose into a perfectly good piece of cloth, then folding and putting it in the pocket for safekeeping, seemed ludicrous. Europeans thought the Natives were astounded by their sailing ships; Natives thought the ships were canoes covered in cobwebs.

Though the work of mapping the coast was arduous, it did not have to be fractious. This latter was largely Vancouver's doing. A combination of ill-health and worries about the ship drove him into increasingly erratic moods that affected everyone. In a letter home, one officer summarized the expedition: "Good health continues in our little squadron, though I am sorry to add not that good fellowship which ought to subsist with adventurers traversing these distance Seas, owing [to] the conduct of our Commander in Chief who is grown Haughty Proud and Insolent, which has kept himself and Officers in a continual state of wrangling during the whole of the Voyage." Near the end of the voyage relations among officers and Vancouver became so strained the captain often dined alone.

The sailors (or "the People," as they were called) were unhappy with Vancouver, too. From their point of view the captain's principal weakness was an inability to recognize the significance of food in their otherwise tedious and barren lives. Besides the regular administrations of "inspissated juice of oranges and lemons" (to prevent scurvy), their diet consisted of salt pork, skilly (salt pork, water and oatmeal) and hardtack. After time, the hardtack became infested with maggots, which, according to sailors of the day, tasted like mustard. On the open ocean, serendipity sometimes delivered variety to the pot, in the form of a pooped-out albatross, or a flying fish. But such gifts were rare. Sailors stuck on the usual fare became so starved for trace minerals that they licked the lubricating fat off the ship's rigging.

On the *Discovery*, the problems with food were the result of the inability or unwillingness of Vancouver to control the cook, twenty-eight-year old John Brown of Dundee. Brown started out on the *Discovery* as a quartermaster then, when the original cook fell ill and was transferred off the ship, he was made "Acting Cook." He was a lousy cook, even by the standards of the day. (A good cook, it was said, was one who knew to place a rotting fish beside biscuits, to draw the maggots out.) Considering Vancouver's concern with scurvy, Brown got away with several mistakes. Once Vancouver caught him skimming the dross from boiled salt pork and selling it to the officers, who smeared the goo on their toast. The renderings were widely (and incorrectly) thought to cause scurvy, and the cook could have expected a lashing. Instead, Vancouver elicited from him a promise to correct his ways. Another time Brown served the crew "pease Soup & pork" into which he accidentally dumped tobacco. Most of the crew, who were smokers, found the dish palatable, if not satisfying, but those who didn't smoke became violently ill. It took the ship's surgeon and naturalist, Archibald Menzies, some detective work before he traced the problem to Brown, who again went unscathed.

The issue of the cook reached a low point when Brown served up a rancid meat dish. The crew complained. Vancouver, who doubled as the ship's purser, ordered the cook to exchange any bowl. According to Hewitt, Brown treated the order with "mockery." A sailor returning a dish of foul food found that Brown simply "changed for a piece out of the same Cask & equally putrid and what the first man brought was given to a 2d complainant in exchange for his & so on. The men on finding this troubled the Purser no more and altho I have seen some of it so highly Putrid as to swim in Water yet they eat it. [T]his was not for want of Provision on Board but for the Emolument of the Purser or the Captain Purser."

And then there was Vancouver's obsession with discipline. Even by the standards of the day, his treatment of crew was harsh. Vancouver disregarded Admiralty orders that limited floggings for summary offences to a dozen lashes. On the *Discovery*, two dozen were common, and three and four dozen not uncommon. No one was immune. Of the one hundred men on board the *Discovery*, sixty were lashed at some time during the voyage. In one ten-month period there were forty-five lashings on the *Discovery*; by comparison, the average on a Royal Navy frigate with a crew of 480 was twenty floggings a year.

Aboard the *Discovery*, the most frequent offences were drunkenness, neglect of duty, insolence, fighting and theft. The usual penalty for fighting was forty-eight

THE *DISCOVERY* AGROUND IN QUEEN CHARLOTTE SOUND. THE SHIP HIT A REEF ON A FALLING TIDE AND WAS THROWN ON ITS STARBOARD SIDE. THE NEXT DAY THE *CHATHAM* GROUNDED. BOTH SHIPS ESCAPED WITHOUT SERIOUS DAMAGE.

lashes; theft, sixty to seventy-two. The record for most lashes went to James Bailey, a twenty-three-year-old seaman from London. He received 144 lashes for desertion. Such a heavy punishment could kill a man, so the flogging was administered in two installments, two weeks apart. The most frequent offender was George Rebold, an armourer, who was flogged at least ten times on the voyage. Rebold, whose offences were insolence and neglect of duty, seems to have been somewhat of an anarchist, willingly trading lashes for the right to tell the officers to, in effect, go to hell.

The *Discovery* was in Frederick Sound, Alaska in September 1794 when charting work was declared done. The crew celebrated with double rations of grog, while Vancouver recorded his joy with the remark that his feelings were "more easily conceived than described." It was apparent, even then, that their

work was of lasting importance. They had set to rest the issue of the Northwest Passage and its attendant fantasies of easy European access to the Orient. They had proved the insularity of Vancouver Island. They had wrested from the Spanish an acknowledgement of Britain's right to a presence on the coast. Vancouver must have been especially pleased that his efforts had replaced speculation and intrigue with hard, intricate detail.

What Vancouver could not have known was the extent to which the meticulous charts, scrolled and stored in the *Discovery*, would dismember Native culture. The charts imposed an empirical form on a coast that for thousands of years had been notionally understood. In London, the maps became the land, and the actual land, the hard thing, was rendered secondary, like a carbon copy for lines drawn on the original. When the *Discovery* sailed away from the Northwest, it took the coast with it, though this would not be apparent for several decades.

After journeying around the Horn, the *Discovery* reached the Kent coast in October, 1795. It was one of the longest voyages in history, both in duration and distance. The ship had been at sea four years, six and a half months. The *Discovery* logged almost 65,000 nautical miles; the small-boat expeditions alone had traversed more than 8,500 nautical miles. The ship was a mass of patched sails and spliced rigging; the crew were ragged and barefoot.

It is a miserable fact of history that Vancouver and the *Discovery* returned to Britain without fanfare. The lack of celebration surrounding Vancouver is attributable, at least in part, to his problems with Pitt. Who, after all, would want to associate with the man who had flogged the prime minister's relative? Furthermore, Pitt seemed bent on revenge, both physically and in the press. He wanted to duel with Vancouver; when they met by chance in a London street, Pitt assaulted him. But Vancouver was

SURGEON AND NATURALIST ARCHIBALD MENZIES OFTEN CLASHED WITH GEORGE VANCOUVER OVER THE EXTENSIVE PLANT COLLECTION HOUSED ON THE *DISCOVERY*'S DECKS. THE RELATIONSHIP WAS COMPLICATED AS VANCOUVER'S HEALTH DETERIORATED AND MENZIES HAD TO TEND TO HIM.

As depicted in this 1796 cartoon, the quarrel-some, former midshipman, Thomas Pitt sought revenge against Vancouver on the streets of London. Pitt is saying, "Give me satisfaction, rascal! Draw your sword, coward! What, you won't? Why then, take that lubber! And that, and that..." Vancouver's reply: "Murder! Murder! Watch Constable, keep him off brother while I run to my Lord Chancellor for protection! Murder! Murder!..."

in no shape for a quarrel. He was feeble, debilitated. He tried a cure at Bristol Hot Springs, but that did not work. Two years after the voyage ended, the Admiralty offered him an ungenerous settlement. He dickered, but poorly. Final payment for the trip: £700, a measly amount for the era. His last work was his journal. Tucked under a duvet, wheezing and tired, he dictated much of his account to his brother, John Vancouver. The account—published as *A Voyage of Discovery to the North Pacific Ocean and Round the World; in which the Coast of North-West America has been Carefully Examined and Accurately Surveyed*—was not quite finished when Vancouver died, on May 12, 1798. He was forty.

The *Discovery* wasted away for some time, too. Then, with Britain and the northern European powers rumbling towards war, it was refitted as a bomb vessel, or monitor. In April 1801, under command of John Conn, a cousin of Lord Nelson, it saw action at the Battle of Copenhagen. The engagement broke the League of Northern Powers, whose embargo on timber threatened British sea power. (It was at Copenhagen that Lord Nelson famously put a telescope to his blind eye and claimed he did not see Admiral Parker's signal to retire.)

After the war, the *Discovery* was decommissioned. Idle until 1808, it was then converted into a prison ship, or hulk, and moored at Sheerness. Charles Dickens could have been describing it when he wrote *Great Expectations*: "[W]e saw the black Hulk lying out a little way from the mud of the shore, like a wicked Noah's ark. Cribbed and barred and moored by massive rusty chains, the prison-ship seemed to be in iron like the prisoners." In 1833, the hull was moved to Deptford, not far from the site of its launch. It languished for a year, then, in February 1834, was broken up.

THE *DISCOVERY* AS A PRISON
SHIP. ACCORDING TO
CHAMBERS' *BOOK OF DAYS*,
"IT WAS AS A MEANS OF
DEVISING A SEVERE MODE OF
PUNISHMENT SHORT OF
DEATH THAT THE HULKS ON
THE THAMES WERE INTRO-
DUCED IN 1776."

Beaver

The rotting, stinking shell of the *Discovery* was still a convict hulk when, in August 1832, George Simpson, the Hudson's Bay Company's governor-in-chief for North America, made an unusual request of his bosses in London. He wanted a steamboat. This odd invention, whose awkward side levers and filthy stacks drew snorts of derision from true sailors, had only been in commercial service two decades. Yet Simpson was sure if such a vessel was stationed at the company post on the Columbia River it would soon reduce transportation costs and eradicate competition.

AFTER EIGHT YEARS AS A SURVEY SHIP, THE *BEAVER* WAS LAID UP BETWEEN INCARNATIONS IN VICTORIA HARBOUR. CAPT. WILLIAM MITCHELL, AN OLD-TIME HUDSON'S BAY COMPANY SKIPPER-CUM-WATCHMAN, LIVED ABOARD THE AGING SHIP AND HOSTED TOURS FOR VISITORS.

The "Little Emperor," as Simpson was called, worded his dispatch in such a way that even the firm's conservative-minded directors could not fault his logic:

> The advantages which a Steam Vessel would possess over sailing craft in navigating the rivers, inlets and sounds, which are so numerous on that coast, and where all the trade is made, embolden us to request that Your Honors will be pleased to provide a Vessel of that description. We are aware that the first cost would be heavy, but we feel assured that she would, in a very short time, become the cheapest craft that could be used, and perform more effective service than any two Sailing Vessels which might be provided...
>
> A Steam Vessel would afford us incalculable advantages over the Americans, as we could look into every Creek and cove while they were confined to harbour by head winds and calms, we could ascend every stream of any consequence upon the coast, we could visit our establishments at stated periods, in short a Steam Vessel would, in our opinion, bring the contest to a close very soon, by making us masters of the trade.

It was typically disingenuous of Simpson to mention American traders. Nothing grated the clubby, monopoly-minded company directors like ruthless Yankee merchants. Wherever furs were to be had, it seemed, "Boston Peddlars" outdealt, undercut and outperformed the HBC. On the Pacific coast the problem was especially acute. Despite a significant HBC post on the Columbia River, Fort George, American free merchants siphoned the bulk of trade, claiming that the Northwest was still an internationally unrecognized area.

Furthermore—and Simpson did not belabour this point in his letter—the steamer might alter the course of the company's money-hemorrhaging Marine Division. The Division was the grandiose name for the little fleet of sailing ships from England that serviced Fort George. Simpson set up the service after discovering—firsthand and nearly disastrously—that the Fraser River was effectively impassable for people or goods. With a dependable overland supply route ruled out, Simpson turned to the sea. As he conceived it, the Marine Division would operate three ships. Mechanical and reliable, they would rotate around the world, profiting at each stop: from Britain to the Columbia with supplies; from the Columbia to China with furs; from China to Britain with tea and spices. The scheme reeked of Simpson's ferocious efficiency.

It was a watertight idea—on paper. Simpson, a true landsman, failed to consider

ONE TRIP DOWN THE INHOS-PITABLE FRASER RIVER WAS ENOUGH TO CONVINCE GEORGE SIMPSON THAT A SEA ROUTE HAD TO BE DEVELOPED TO PROVISION HUDSON'S BAY COMPANY COASTAL POSTS.

the vagaries of the sea and seamen. Sailing ships, in particular, were vulnerable to eddies and currents that litter the coast. With no source of power independent of the wind, which was often onshore, the ships had no way to extricate themselves from dangerous situations. The first victim was the *William and Ann*, which was wrecked on the bar in March 1829; the brig *Isabella* disintegrated after hitting the Columbia River bar on her maiden voyage; in 1834 the oak sloop *Vancouver* was destroyed on Rose Spit in the Queen Charlotte Islands. In each case, the disasters were attributable to a treacherous combination of strong currents and adverse winds.

The situation on the coast was so bad some sailing ship captains flouted orders. Before the *William and Ann* was wrecked, Captain Henry Hanwell took the little brig on a trading mission. Hanwell, who was used to trading out of Hudson Bay, was supposed to explore the recesses of the coast in search of furs. After several bad experiences, he tucked into Observatory Inlet, where he stayed twenty-nine days. Natives wanting to trade had to come to him. He was too afraid to even explore the head of the inlet. His total haul: thirty-seven beaver, five river or land otter skins.

Slack, inept and drunken skippers plagued the company's marine department for years. Simpson met one of these during a visit to the Pacific coast. In his journal he wrote: "Captn Davidsons talent as a Navigator I know nothing about, but his talent as a Grog Drinker I understand is without parallel and I shall be agreeably surprised if he and his Ship ever reach the Port of Destination." Captain Davidson, as a matter of record, did make a safe passage. But another troublesome mariner, Captain L.J. Hayne of the *Ganymede*, did not. While on the coast, Hayne was frequently observed to be "free with Liquor." He drank before breakfast; he drank in the evening. No one saw him sober. Soon after leaving the coast, Hayne became unhinged and ordered his ship to Hobart, Tasmania.

Simpson had hoped that the ships of the Marine Division would be a "presence" in the Northwest, a powerful symbol of the HBC. But in this, too, he misjudged the nature of the coast. By the turn of the eighteenth century, Natives had seen enough sailing ships to distinguish British from American, a brig from a schooner. Any residual wonders they may have had concerning the European vessels' propulsion systems were dispelled by frequent crack-ups. Simpson recognized that the HBC ships would have little impact on the Natives when he saw the size and agility of their own craft. Small vessels like the *Cadboro*, he wrote, are "quite unfit for the Trade, there are hundreds of War Canoes on the Coast, longer and higher out of the water...carrying from 40 to 50 men each."

In 1836, Simpson got his steamer. The *Beaver* was the same length as the *Discovery*, but fitted with a steam engine and side paddle wheels as well as masts. It sailed from England to the Columbia River under Captain David Horne, a studious seaman who insisted on daily prayer. Two days after it sailed up the Columbia, its sidewheels, shipped for the voyage, were installed, steam was brought up in the boiler, and the *Beaver* moved down the river to the Pacific. It did not stop working the coast for fifty-two years.

The *Beaver*! The little black ship! The stout ship! The good ship! The ship that carried James Douglas to Victoria! The ship that quelled the Indians! The ship that carried a funny old bear! The steamer played so many roles—trading vessel, passenger ship, freighter, tug, survey ship, gunboat—for such a long time, that its chunky form and the resonant thud, thud, thud of its wheels are inseparable from BC history. If something important happened in BC in the mid-1800s, chances are the *Beaver* carried it or shot at it. The *Beaver* carried settlers, soldiers, gold seekers, missionaries. It towed log booms and sailing ships. It helped map a thousand miles of BC coast (often the hard way, by "finding" rocks and reefs with the hull). It was burned, sunk, salvaged, rebuilt. By the time its career ended in 1888, the *Beaver* seemed more like a fleet than a lone little ship.

The *Beaver* endured because it was strong. It was built in the spring of 1835 by Green, Wigram and Green at the Blackwell yard on the River Thames. Blackwell was one of the true institutions of British shipbuilding. In 1588, the yard-built craft helped destroy the Spanish Armada. Their versions of the swift, luxurious East Indiamen were regarded as the *ne plus ultra* of the shipping world. This shipbuilding tradition was apparent in the *Beaver*. Into its hull went a forest of woods: African oak, tropical greenheart, British oak and elm, red pine and Norwegian pine. The keel was a massive cant of oak, the ribs stout pieces of carefully dressed oak and greenheart. The outside planking was oak and elm, fastened with oak treenails and copper bolts. Over this was laid tarred paper, followed by a layer of thick fir planking, spiked with bronze nails. The hull was sheathed in copper. According to the original Certificate of Registry, the ship was "Well constructed and workmanship generally of the best quality." Half a century later, divers working on the submerged hull found that wood under the sheathing was as sound as the day it was launched.

The *Beaver*'s steam engines were equally sturdy. It had two; they weighed 32 tons apiece. Each produced 35 nominal horsepower. They were called noncondensing engines, because steam vented from the cylinder went up the exhaust instead of returning to the boiler (as it would in later steam engines). Noncondensing engines used a lot of water and made a loud, hollow sound, like blowing across an empty bottle. The boilers—big rectangular boxes—sat atop the fireboxes. Though rated for 5 pounds pressure, the boilers often worked at 2.5 pounds, sometimes less. One engineer claimed the ship could "run on a vacuum." It was not a powerful ship; even when new it could not blow the whistle and spin the 13-foot-diameter sidewheels at the same time. In later years, it wasn't unusual to see the *Beaver*, wheels churning like a freestyle swimmer, being pushed astern by an adverse current.

The *Beaver* had many incarnations; the first, and most important was as a fur trader. This time, Simpson got it right. The *Beaver* was a huge improvement on the vulnerable sailing ships. Its hold loaded with merchandise, it steamed along the coast from Puget Sound to Russian Alaska, stopping at Native settlements to trade. On the North Coast, especially, it did a booming business. According to the ship's log for April 10 to 14, 1837, while the *Beaver* was trading on the Nass River, the following were received: "32 large beaver, 13 small beaver, 20 large land otter, 3 black bear, 152 marten, 1 fisher, 31 mink and 1 American sea otter pup."

In return, the traders handed out the following: "6 gills of powder, 6 bunches blue cut glass beads, 36 strings of same, 42 yards salampore, 2 small black silk hankerchiefs, 8 turkey hankys, 138 gallons rum, 15 tin pans, 1 pannikin, 2 pint pots, 5 pounds vermillion, 8 yards brown cotton, 272 heads tobacco, 14 yards 'G.P' cotton, 1 tin kettle, 5 gills black shot, 6 3-point blue blankets, 3 2-point blue blankets, 2 yards of duffle, 2 3-point red blankets and 2 gallons molasses."

What Natives thought of the *Beaver*—the first steamer on the coast—is largely unrecorded. HBC traders liked to think the ship's machinery was, literally, awe-inspiring. They pointed to the quick incorporation of the vessel in local iconography—in a petroglyph and on a totem pole, depicting one of its captains. John Dunn, an HBC trader and author of an early history, was on board when the *Beaver* first arrived in Fort McLoughlin (near present-day Bella Bella). Some Natives, he wrote, "were greatly surprised when they saw the steam boat, saying she could do anything but speak; and that the white man must have been assisted in the work by the Great Spirit." But Dunn also records that other Natives thought the craft had more earthly origins and vowed to make their own version. They felled a large cedar, then hollowed out a section about 30 feet (9 m) long. Fire blacking was smeared on the hull and the deck covered with hand-split planks. The crew concealed themselves under the decking and, rotating red paddles, powered the facsimile around in circles. "She was floated triumphantly," wrote Dunn, "and went at the rate of three miles an hour."

But the *Beaver*'s independence from sail and paddle came at a price. Feeding the voracious appetites of the boilers required the efforts of fourteen woodcutters. It took two days of cutting to keep the ship going for a single day. Twenty-six cords supplied it for two or three days. Fully loaded with wood, the *Beaver* had little room for cargo; fully loaded with cargo, it had little room for wood. Towing log booms—a later occupation—used even more fuel: forty cords in twenty-four hours. It was only when the *Beaver* was fed coal that it could make longer journeys between refuellings. Even then it devoured 700 pounds of coal an hour.

As the flagship of the HBC's empire on the coast, the *Beaver* was buffed and polished to a blinding shine. Dr. J.S. Helmcken left an account of a visit to the ship in 1850:

> We went outside the fort and there lay the *Beaver*, Captain Dodd in command, so clean, so nice, so spruce, with boarding nettings all round, cannon on deck, muskets and cutlasses arranged in their proper places, beautiful cabins, and good furniture, with a trading place for Indians, who I was told, were only allowed a few at a time on board, when on trade. She had a large crew...active, robust, weather-beaten, jolly, good-tempered men...fat, from not being

(TOP) THE *BEAVER*'S HOUSEWORK WAS CUT DOWN AND IT WAS TRANSFORMED INTO A TOWBOAT AND CARGO SHIP. IT TOOK FOURTEEN WOODCUTTERS TWO DAYS TO PRODUCE ENOUGH WOOD TO KEEP THE SHIP RUNNING FOR A SINGLE DAY.

(BOTTOM) CAPTAIN CHARLES DODD CAME FROM ENGLAND TO SERVE AS FIRST MATE ON THE *BEAVER*, AND HE COMMANDED THE SHIP FROM 1845 TO 1851.

overworked; some grey, some grizzled, some young; the former had once been similar to the latter in the service.

For the *Beaver*'s second incarnation, as gunboat, consider the following scenario. A shepherd is killed at Christmas Hill in Saanich. Two Indians, one from Cowichan, one from Nanaimo, are accused. Settlers wail for justice. Chief Factor James Douglas loads the *Beaver* with 130 seamen and steams north. One Native is arrested in Cowichan. In Nanaimo, the other accused spots the *Beaver* snorting past Jack Point and heads for the woods. Sixteen seamen and nine "half whites" off the ship give chase. The accused is caught in a thicket. A trial is held on the decks of the *Beaver*. Douglas is judge, officers the jury. The deliberation is short, the verdicts: guilty. The two convicts are taken from the ship to nearby Protection Island. On January 17, 1853, in front of the men, women and children of the local tribe, the two are hung. Several days later the *Beaver* returns to duty as a trading vessel.

It was through such gunboat excursions—usually brief and violent—that the *Beaver* was used as an agent of empire. Its physical versatility complemented the prevailing notion that justice must be swift as well as harsh—especially when Indians were involved. The threat of Native revolt was very real in the mid-1800s, and Douglas was never reluctant to use steam and cannon to back his authority.

In this role, the *Beaver* was similar to dozens of small steamers—armed and unarmed—working for European empires around the world in the nineteenth and early twentieth centuries. The most famous of these are C.S. Forester's *The African Queen* and the black-flanked steamer in Joseph Conrad's novella, *Heart of Darkness*. Small, nimble and shallow of draft, they carried on the work of colonization begun by bigger ocean-going warships. These "handy tools of empire," as one historian called them, took European customs, laws and goods up and down river into the farthest reaches of new lands.

The *Beaver* was also cast as a passenger vessel. Though fitted to carry cargo rather than people, it was used as a ferry when needed. The discovery of gold on the Fraser River in 1857 created such a demand. Victoria was soon overflowing with eager gold seekers, desperate to get to the gold fields. One of the passengers was Charles H. Woodward, who left an account of the journey to Fort Langley:

> The *Beaver* was one of the earliest experiments in marine steamship architecture, constructed apparently more with a view to carry freight than passengers. At all events, if there were any comfortable cabin accommodations, none of my party were fortunate enough to gain access, much less to occupy them. We stood huddled together for mutual warmth on the after-deck like cattle, and indeed with less provision for our comfort than is nowadays provided for cattle. A small awning covered but half the deck passengers, and afforded but little protection against a heavy driving storm of sleet and snow which followed us from start to finish, while those unable to get positions under it had no protection. Fortunately the only redeeming feature of the trip was its brevity, but it was long enough to impress a lasting memory of its discomforts, and it stands unrivalled as the smallest voyage with the largest amount of discomfort in all my experience...

FREQUENT INDIAN ATTACKS ON SETTLERS IN AMERICAN TERRITORY PROMPTED JAMES DOUGLAS TO USE THE *BEAVER* AS A GUNBOAT.

The *Beaver*'s incarnation as a towboat began on its first day of work on the coast, May 17, 1836. According to the ship's log:

> At daylight unmoored ship and got the steam up. At 3:30 weighed and ran down abreast of the lower plain for firewood. At noon lashed alongside the *Columbia*. At 1:30 took the *Columbia* in tow up to the saw-mill. At 6 returned and anchored off Fort Vancouver in 5 fathoms.

In its later years especially, towing was the *Beaver*'s staple, the rent cheque, the bussing job it did nights to pay for the fun stuff during the day. In October 1874 the HBC sold the *Beaver* to a group of Victoria businessmen. The price was $15,700. They hacked off deckwork, installed a tow bit and operated as the BC Towing and Transportation Company. The *Beaver* ranged all over the coast looking for work—towing log booms out of the Stikine River, scows between Vancouver and Victoria. It fetched wind-bound sailing ships from Juan de Fuca Strait and yarded them to Departure Bay in Nanaimo. As long as it wasn't pressed against a strong current it did its work capably; otherwise, there was trouble. In the early 1880s, the *Beaver* was in Juan de Fuca Strait when it took the sailing ship *Henry Buck* in tow. The *Henry Buck* was a coal carrier, bound for Departure Bay. When the *Beaver* and its tow arrived at Dodd Narrows—a capillary-sized waterway between Vancouver Island and Mudge Island—the current was still ebbing. Instead of waiting for flood, the captain tried to power through. The current snatched the *Beaver*'s bow and spun it like a weather vane in a shifting wind—straight into the *Henry Buck*. The collision jarred both craft,

THE RUGGED AND STURDY
BEAVER DID EVERYTHING
FROM LUGGING BOOM
CHAINS TO TRANSPORTING
HARD-SCRABBLE SETTLERS

but did no damage to the bigger sailing ship. The *Beaver*, however, was crippled. The smokestack fell off with a clatter, and the wheel bearing on one paddle wheel cracked and disappeared with a splash. Helpless, both vessels dropped anchors. Another steamer took the *Henry Buck* to Nanaimo, then returned and towed the lame *Beaver* to Victoria.

Aging hull decorated with a thousand rock-caused rosebuds, the *Beaver* laboured in the 1880s at jobs no other vessel wanted. It lugged boom chains north to logging camps or hard-scrabble settlers to Valdez Island. Once, it was called upon to move a Vancouver bear to Victoria. The bear was owned by George Black, a Gastown butcher. Black had bought the bear, as a cub, from a man who shot its mother in New Westminster. He kept it tied with a collar and chain to a dock. After several years he tired of the bear and sold it to Goodacre & Dooley's Market in Victoria. Why he did this is not clear; the sale may have been related to feeding costs. It is on record that the bear ate forty-two pigs in three years.

The bear was tied to the deck of the *Beaver*. On the journey to Victoria it broke loose. Though accounts vary, it appears the animal entered the ship's galley and startled a fireman and the French-Canadian cook. The fireman dove down a fiddley—one of the periscope-shaped vents leading to the engine room. The cook, somewhat calmer, used a bowl of sugar to entice the bear to put its head through a porthole. By then the crew were alerted to a problem with the cargo. While the bear slurped the sugar, the crew bound its body with rope. This time, there was no chance the bear would regain its freedom. When it was slaughtered and skinned the next day, the rope marks were still visible on the carcass.

On the evening of July 26, 1888, the *Beaver* finished loading at Vancouver's City Wharf and cast off. It was bound for Thurlow Island with logging supplies. At the wheel, Captain George Marchant, a bulbous-nosed veteran of local waters and watering holes, struggled to make out the passage through First Narrows, his vision impaired by alcohol and fog. In the midst of the narrows, the ship was caught in an eddy and spun onto what is now known as Prospect Point. According to one story, the crew stayed aboard, then rowed back to Vancouver in the morning. According to another, they made their way through the park, back to the Sunnyside Saloon they had left. In any case, they were not harmed, but the *Beaver*'s career as a work boat was finished. Old and underpowered, it did not warrant salvage and repair. The owners opted to say goodbye to the ship and left it on the rocks.

Like pigs and saints, the *Beaver* was more revered in death than life. Its wood rotting, iron weeping rust, the hulk remained on the rocks for several years. A group of Vancouver businessmen declared the wreck to be of international significance and tried to raise funds to send it to the Chicago World's Fair. The plan failed. The Cates family, who owned a well-known towing company, had a notion to set the hulk ashore as a monument. That, too, went nowhere. A local building mover, Charles W. McCain, saw some quick cash in the boiler's masses of copper and had it removed, but his partner, Henry Brown, lost his life in the salvage. (Superstitious seamen said the *Beaver* wasn't going to give up its treasures easily.)

GEORGE MARCHANT, SOME-TIME MASTER OF NEARLY EVERY TURN-OF-THE-CENTURY TOWBOAT, WAS ABOARD THE *BEAVER* ON ITS FINAL RUN. IN 1902, WHEN THE RECENTLY LAUNCHED TUG *SUPERIOR* SANK WHILE UNDER MARCHANT'S COMMAND, A NEWSPAPER QUIPPED THAT THE OLD MARINER HAD SUCCEEDED IN SINKING THE COAST'S OLDEST AND NEWEST VESSELS.

CANADIAN PACIFIC
RAILWAY'S *EMPRESS OF
INDIA* PASSES THE WRECK OF
THE *BEAVER* OFF PROSPECT
POINT.

Meanwhile the relic had become part of the Vancouver scene, an early version of a maritime museum, where souvenir hunters and tourists and old-timers could gather and gaze or throw rocks at the pioneer steamer of the Pacific Northwest. But slowly, surely, the sea claimed the wreck. On July 26, 1892, the swell from the sidewheeler *Yosemite* dislodged the ship's enormous boiler, which tumbled into the channel with large parts of the hull. A few remnants of the old ship remained visible at low tide. By 1894 there was nothing to be seen.

McCain had recognized the historic interest in the *Beaver* and used some of the copper to mint three different sizes of commemorative medallions. The medallions went quickly, as did the counterfeits that appeared. Soon, other souvenirs drifted onto the scene: walking sticks, picture frames, furniture, furniture inlays, cribbage

boards, cups, boxes, toys and jewellery. The *Beaver*'s wheel showed up, then another. The same thing happened with the ship's bells. By 1990 there existed at least four "authentic" bells, and rumours hinted at more. A century after it vanished beneath the waves, the *Beaver* is still making history.

ITS HULL BATTERED AND ITS
BOLTS WEEPING RUST, THE
BEAVER PERCHED ON THE
ROCKS FOR SEVERAL YEARS
BEFORE TUMBLING INTO THE
DEEP.

William Irving

I n the early 1860s, British author R. Byron Johnson was travelling up the Fraser River on a sternwheeler bound for Hope. A youthful wanderer, as familiar with the outposts of the British Empire as he was with the lampposts of Piccadilly Circus, Johnson was in the colony of British Columbia to observe the frenzied carnival of the gold rush. Since the river had panned out yellow in 1858, the colony had been swarmed by fortune-seekers, hucksters, snake-oil salesmen and fellow adventurers—just the sort of crowd that piqued Johnson's interest.

THE *WILLIAM IRVING* ON THE FRASER RIVER. A GREAT ADVAN-
TAGE OF STERNWHEELERS OVER SIDEWHEELERS WAS THEIR
ABILITY TO NOSE ALONGSIDE A RIVERBANK. JOHN IRVING'S
GILDED EAGLE PERCHES ABOVE THE WHEELHOUSE—HIS
DECLARATION OF THE SHIP'S SUPREMACY.

Johnson and dozens of other passengers were strolling the decks when a rival riverboat was spotted astern. It was gaining. Leaning from his wheelhouse window, the captain of Johnson's boat hollered down to the engineer for more steam. The two vessels, resembling self-propelled wedding cakes, flailed upstream. Still the rival gained. The captain bellowed. Desperate for fuel, the engineer ripped open the cargo. According to Johnson, "Several sacks of bacon were thrown into the flames, making them roar like a strong east wind. Up went the steam gauge till it showed 160 lbs to the square inch, just 40 more than was allowed by the government certificate, framed and glazed in the cabin." The engineer jabbed a filthy finger at the gauge in alarm, but the captain was unfazed. "[T]he old boat's never bin whipped yet," he bawled, "and ain't going to be till she busts!"

Moments later Johnson's ship was impaled on a snag raking from the bank. The snag punched through the hull and a heap of cargo, and pierced a horse. While crew plugged the hull with blankets snatched from passengers, the rival steamboat tooted past—without, recorded the indignant Johnson, "stopping to see if we were sinking or not." The leaking ship was run aground on a nearby sandbar, where passengers stayed for two long days, smacking mosquitoes and watching steamers pass by. Johnson had never seen anything like it.

Neither, for that matter, had the residents of the colony. As part of the route from Victoria to the gold fields, the once lonely river was now a major highway, crowded with canoes, homemade dugouts and, most glamorously, riverboats. Flat-bottomed, shallow-draft and well-liquored, riverboats shunted passengers and supplies from Victoria and New Westminster, up the Fraser River 95 nautical miles to the head of navigation at Yale, where prospectors followed the 12-foot-wide (4 m) wagon road 400 miles (640 km) to the Cariboo. The boats were run by flamboyant, to-hell-with-the-rules men like Johnson's captain, or the forgotten skipper who said of his ship, "she's fine for passengers, but I wouldn't trust treasure in her." The riverboats were the rush to the Fraser's gold.

Riverboats often worked in water that wouldn't float a log. Some registered their draft in inches. "My boat can sail on a heavy dew," was the sort of thing a steamboater boasted. One skipper claimed his ship went aground in ankle-deep water on gravel ridged by spawning salmon. Another told a story about a passenger who, panicked by the boat's proximity to the shore, jumped overboard. He landed with a thud.

When a sandbar blocked a steamer's way, the captain turned the ship around

CAPT. WILLIAM IRVING LEARNED THE ART OF STEAM-BOATING ON THE COLUMBIA RIVER, WHERE STERNWHEEL-ERS DESCENDING THE RIVER THROUGH THE CASCADES WERE CLOCKED AT 90 KM/H OVER SHORT DISTANCES.

and used the revolving paddles to "walk" it, stern first, over the bar into deep water. If that didn't work, then the crew deployed a block-and-tackle device called a grasshopper, and the ship hoisted itself over the obstruction. Nothing stopped them. The sternwheeler *Skuzzy*, aided by 150 Chinese labourers who pulled a line from shore, steamed through Hells Gate, a 100-foot-wide (30 m) rock-lined slit that forced the mighty Fraser off its belly and slid it sideways for several hundred yards. The river's surge through the gorge reached 100,000 cubic feet per second (2,830 m³/sec). Other steamers, assembled above Hells Gate, wormed and muscled their way, like cardiovascular probes, into the province's interior, plying as far as Takla Lake. They carried pianos for frontier hotels, rails for the railroads. They did the impossible, and they did it profitably.

Steamboats plied the Fraser River from 1858 until the turn of the century, thriving on gold, a rail-building boom, settlement of the Fraser valley. At various times the business was dominated by different vessels, but none ruled the river with such aplomb as the *William Irving*. At 166 feet, half again as long as the *Beaver*, the *William Irving* was the flagship of the Pioneer Line, one of the feistier steam lines that fought for mastery of the river.

The *William Irving* was launched in Burrard Inlet in 1880. It was named after the founder of the Pioneer Line, a Scotsborn, deep-sea trained Columbia River skipper who came north for the gold rush. William Irving built several stern- or sidewheelers, ran them hard, and prospered. A true seaman, he was never comfortable with the locally trained riverboaters' landlubberly habits, such as calling the stack a chimney. When he paced around his home in New Westminster, he did so to the exact dimensions of a wheelhouse. When his son, John, was just a boy William set him

to learning the seaman's language: a bellowed "press sail!" meant hurry; "clear the ship" was code for take it easy. On the river, Irving pointed out the riffles and boils that marked underwater hazards, taught John to see a safe passage through whitewater rocks. He had the kid reading the river before most children were tying their own shoelaces.

William Irving died in 1872, leaving John to take over. Though just seventeen, John was already over 6 feet tall, and had the handsome demeanour of a man two decades his senior. John had plenty of ideas for expanding the company, most of them contingent on driving competition from the river. In particular, John wanted to get rid of Bill Moore, an obnoxiously resilient rival steamboater who ran a variety of

CONVIVIAL, HARD-HEADED, SKILLED AND A "TWO-FISTED DRINKER," WILLIAM IRVING'S SON JOHN WAS THE CONSUMMATE RIVERBOATER.

sternwheelers out of Victoria under a variety of corporate incarnations. Moore's periodic challenges to the Pioneer Line inevitably resulted in lower freights, races and reduced profits. There were other competitors, too: Captain Fleming and Captain Otis Parsons jointly operated the *Hope* and the *Lillooet*; Captain Millard ran the diminutive *Gem*, also known as "Coalscuttle" or "Hog-pen."

As the premier steamboaters, both Moore and Irving were supported by their respective city's newspapers. Championing Moore for his efforts to keep the accident-prone Irving ships from gaining too strong a purchase on the river, the Victoria papers dubbed New Westminster a "pimple on the face of creation." New Westminster lauded Irving, and said any city "built on a frog pond" deserved the reckless Moore.

In truth, no slander would have been inaccurate—for the men or the cities. Both entrepreneurs abhorred competition, and worked hard to get rid of it. In 1877 the Irvings offered to pay Moore to leave the river for a year. He accepted and rates went through the wheelhouse roof. Neither steamboater could boast an unblemished safety record. With top cargo prices going to vessels first up the river, engineers were told to ignore government pressure regulations. "More steam!" was the rally call of a generation of steamboaters.

In 1879, with work on the long-awaited Canadian Pacific Railway line to Vancouver due to begin, John Irving ordered a new steamer built. The *William Irving* was to be the finest and most luxurious sternwheeler on the river. It was launched on March 18, 1880. In its basic form—boxy, triple-decked, built on a flat-bottomed hull with unhandsomely swept bow—the *William Irving* resembled many other steamers on the Fraser. The main deck was reserved for the dirty work: the boiler, firebox, engine room, cargo and kitchen. Above that were passenger cabins, dining rooms, salons. From the upper deck rose the wheelhouse, 40 feet above the water.

What distinguished the ship, however, was the finishing work. Crowned by Irving's trademark gilt eagle on the wheelhouse roof, the ship was as ornate as a gingerbread house. Fine woodwork and luxurious furniture adorned the salons. Silver settings graced linen-covered tables in the dining room. A prime feature was the cabin furniture, which Irving boasted in an advertisement featured "patent spring mattresses" and were "of comfortable dimensions." The ship cost Irving $75,000, a fantastic sum when a working man was doing well to make three dollars a day.

"Capt. John Irving may well feel proud of his new venture," reported the *Inland Sentinel* after the *William Irving*'s first run up the Fraser:

> She sits upon the water like a duck, and moves as a thing of life, breasting the swiftest current without hesitancy. The boat is finished in the best possible style for pleasure and durability. Upon her first trip she was accompanied by the Royal City Band, discoursing appropriate responses to honors paid. The 'Boys' had a good time, and gratified many persons who were reminded of the charms of music in the other days.

Captain John set the *William Irving* against Moore, whose latest corporate incarnation was called the People's Steamboat Line, and an upstart outfit from Cassiar running a former Moore boat, the *Gertrude*. All three outfits were vying for work supplying the railroad—lugging steel or Chinese labourers from New Westminster to Yale. Prices tumbled, tempers rose. The instinct to press a boat beyond its limits was overwhelming. On one occasion Moore was caught running 140 pounds of steam pressure, 40 more than the maximum. He was fined $200 and pilloried in the ever-hostile New Westminster press: "[Moore's] steamer *Western Slope* has certainly enjoyed a remarkable run of success during the greater part of this season... sailing through Dominion statutes with as much assurance as she would run over a luckless fisherman's net." Competition reduced the upriver journey from twelve hours to ten; then the steamers turned and hurtled downriver in five hours.

    With its great paddle wheels and powerful engine, the *William Irving* dominated the trade. Even when a rival boat got away from the New Westminster docks early, the *Irving* soon caught up. There was a thrill of excitement as it nosed past the rival, Captain John searching the current for the kick of an eddy that might propel the boat ever faster. Then, just when the thrashing paddles were clear of the rival's bow, *Irving* pulled impudently in front and steamed ahead to Mission.

    Mission was where Charlie lived. Charlie was the old horse who opened the bridge crossing the river. When he heard a ship's whistle he walked on his own to the centre of the bridge tracks and plodded around and around on a sweep. The bridge was supposed to be out of the way by the time the ship arrived, but with Charlie's sore feet and aching joints, it was usually slow to fully open. While the *William Irving* waited for Charlie, the competitor caught up. Then the race began anew.

    Competition on the river reached a pitch in the fall of 1882. On a Sunday, the *William Irving* and the *Gertrude* were both headed downriver for Langley. As they came alongside, both captains ordered on steam. They jockeyed on their big ships, seeking to get the best position in the river. Suddenly, before the passengers lining the observation decks could bellow "watch out," the current brought the two vessels together. There was a shriek of iron grinding against iron, a rip of splintering wood. The ship's guardrails locked, and the coupled vessels spun downstream, their skippers straining to separate them. Loyal passengers from rival boats hollered face to face. After several minutes, the ships sheared off. As the *Irving* limped away, someone on the

MONEYED TRAVELLERS JOURNEYED THE FRASER RIVER IN LUXURY. PICTURED HERE IS A LOUNGE IN THE *WILLIAM IRVING*'S SISTER SHIP, THE *R.P. RITHET*.

Gertrude splatted an egg on the *Irving*'s wheelhouse window.

"The rivalry on the river is becoming fast and furious," admonished the *Victoria Colonist*, "and we would advise caution on all sides, for should a disaster occur, a terrible responsibility will attach somewhere." But damaged boats, fines and impossible competition were too much for Moore; before the year was out he was bankrupt. The *William Irving* ruled the river.

Hair spiked with dry sweat, shoes slathered in mud, a young riverboater named T.S. Guns hobbled into the offices of the *New Westminster Columbian* one morning in 1893 and announced he had a story to tell about John Irving. A reporter found him a chair, folded a notebook to a clean page and picked up a pencil. Here's what Guns said:

> I just want to tell you what happened to fourteen deck hands... We shipped aboard at Victoria on Monday, anchored all night at the mouth of the river, and at 6 o'clock yesterday morning weighed anchor and pulled alongside the Garry Point cannery. We loaded salmon at one or two canneries, and then came direct to Westminster, where we went to work loading on 3,000 sacks of grain for Victoria. We worked till supper time and immediately afterwards were put to work again at loading, and kept at it till one o'clock in the morning, but were ordered not to turn in as it was expected we should go down river to load salmon at Ewen's cannery. At five o'clock this morning [we] sailed, and about six o'clock drew alongside the cannery. The planks were run ashore, and we were ordered to go ahead loading. Well, when a fellow has been working all night, he should get his breakfast in the morning before going to work, and the fourteen of us made up our minds we were going to get our breakfast, and said so. Captain Irving got mad and ordered us all ashore, and there we marched over the plank, without a cent of pay, and... with the dunnage of nearly all still aboard. Look at that (showing his trowsers legs covered with Lulu Island mud). We all had to march up to the city on the Lulu Island dyke, and here I am without a cent in my pocket and thirteen other chaps in the same fix.

THE *GERTRUDE*, OPERATED BY IRVING'S ARCH-RIVAL, CAPT. BILL MOORE, WORKED THE STIKINE AND FRASER RIVERS.

As Guns discovered, the convivial, colourful Irving could be a bastard to work for. Lowly deckhands especially bore the brunt of his scorn. Theirs was a filthy job,

sometimes wrestling obstinate cattle aboard the *William Irving*, other times trundling cases of salmon or sacks of flour. To make matters worse, Irving often hired according to race, then pitted an all-Native shift against an all-white shift. The pay was minimal, the work never-ending. Sleep, like meals, was something to be grabbed, collapsed on a haystack. To caution young men from considering a decking job, veterans often told them about another newcomer who signed on to the *William Irving*. He was finishing his first day of work. "When do we sleep?" he wearily asked a fellow deckhand. "Don't know," was the tired reply. "I only joined the boat three days ago."

Nor were passengers exempt from Irving's ill treatment. Wealthy and reckless, he permitted most travellers on his boats, but not all. Men of the cloth, in particular, seem to have raised his ire. Once the *William Irving* was loading at the Chilliwack dock when Captain John spotted a clergyman about to board. Leaning from the wheelhouse, he hollered to the mate to stop the parson. The parson looked up inquisitively and asked why. Clergymen and a grey mare, Captain John shouted down, should not travel together. He had carried such a combination three times before, and on each occasion there was trouble. And since there was already a grey mare on the main deck, on this trip, at least, there would be no parsons. The clergyman objected, but he might as well have talked to a cold boiler. He was left standing on the wharf.

WHILE THE *WILLIAM IRVING* PROFITED ON THE LOWER FRASER RIVER FROM THE RAIL-BUILDING BOOM, IT WAS THE *SKUZZY* WHICH BECAME FAMOUS FOR MAKING IT THROUGH THE FRENZIED WATERS OF HELLS GATE— WITH ASSISTANCE FROM 150 CHINESE WORKERS.

THE PIONEER LINE'S *R.P. RITHET* AT YALE, EFFECTIVELY THE END OF THE FRASER RIVER'S NAVIGABLE WATERS FOR BIG RIVER STEAMERS. NOTE THE GATHERING AT THE END OF THE STREET.

On its bi-weekly run along the Fraser River from New Westminster to Yale, the *William Irving* often steamed for hours without a stop. It made scheduled dockings at Mission and Chilliwack or put in at a private wharf if a white flag was flown. Passengers drank and ate in the dining room, or stood on the decks and watched the riverbank cottonwoods sliding by. It was one of the delights of riverboat travel, with the rhythmic splash, splash of the paddle wheels a distant noise astern, that a man leaning on the railing could pass a few friendly words with a boy fishing from the bank. A woman perched on a deck bench could hear the metallic snick, snick of a farmer's horse-drawn sickle-bar mower in a nearby field. Steamboat smells mixed with the fragrance of ripe blackberries. As long as the vessel wasn't involved in a dangerous race, it could be a glorious, civilized ride through the country.

The *William Irving* was wrecked at the end of June 1894. Though still run by

Irving, it was now officially registered to the Canadian Pacific Navigation Company, a conglomerate formed in 1883 by the merger of Irving's Pioneer Line with the fleet of the Hudson's Bay Company. The *Irving* was loaded with cattle and freight and headed downriver when Captain John brought it alongside a disabled sister ship, the *R.P. Rithet*. The *Rithet* had broken a shaft two days earlier at Maria Slough, and needed a tow. The two ships were lashed together and slipped into the stream. Everything went well until they reached Farr's Bluff, where the current swept the vessels around. Out of control, the *William Irving* slammed bow first into the rocky shore, taking the full force of the *R.P. Rithet*. It clung to the rocks for several moments, then tore loose. With timbers strained and shattered, it spun downstream to a sandbar. As a newspaper of the day reported, when "she touched bottom her back broke...A COMPLETE WRECK!"

The loss was major, but not catastrophic. Much of the high-profit railway work had already vanished with the completion of the transcontinental line. The lucrative job of hauling produce to the Admiralty's naval base at Esquimalt was about to disappear, too, for the British were transferring the base to the much smaller Canadian navy. The riverboat era was waning. By 1909, most of the riverboats were gone.

ITS TIMBERS SHATTERED BY THE COLLISION AT FARR'S BLUFF, THE *WILLIAM IRVING* WAS SWEPT DOWNSTREAM AND LODGED ON A SANDBAR.

Lorne

After the euphoric, loose-moneyed days of the gold rush, the 1880s seemed like a nickel-and-dime era of hard work and frustration. The wealth of natural resources was there, all right, but how to get at it? Railroaders punched lines through improbable passes, only to see tracks carried away in landslides. Loggers laboured for days to free single trees from the forest. Settlers battled floods, miners worked unproven rock. To myriad exhausted, broke and dismayed pioneers, the promises of BC's wealth appeared to be locked in an impregnable glass case.

Even when they did wrest timber, ore and produce from the land, there remained the problem of getting goods to market. BC, then as now, relied on exports. Yet international shipping companies were loath to dispatch vessels to the Northwest. The problem was primarily the entrance to Juan de Fuca Strait, the 12-nautical-mile-wide channel marked by Washington state's Cape Flattery in the south and the sweeping, rock-strewn west coast of Vancouver Island to the north. It was through this strait that deep-sea ships headed to or from the burgeoning inland ports had to pass.

THE MIGHTY TUG *LORNE*, OFF THE MOUTH OF
THE CAPILANO RIVER, C. 1925.

To navigators unfamiliar with the strait, the transit looked unexacting. A sailing vessel would approach from the west, with the prevailing wind astern. When the finger of Cape Flattery was cleared, the ship altered course to the southeast and sailed into the strait. Off Victoria the ship either turned south into Puget Sound or, if it was bound for Departure Bay or Burrard Inlet, heave to and wait for a tow through the wormy passes of the Gulf Islands.

A number of factors could turn this plan into disaster. Foremost, in the days of sail, was wind. With the great fetch of the Pacific, winds regularly reached the coast at speeds of 55 knots. At Tatoosh Island, off Cape Flattery, winds in excess of Beaufort 7 (33 knots) are recorded nineteen days or more each month in winter. As many sailing ship captains discovered, a fair onshore wind off the coast of Washington transformed into an offshore wind at the entrance to the strait. This was a result of inland geography, which funnelled wind past Olympia, in southern Washington, through Puget Sound, and out the strait, where it ran headlong into the parent wind. Many square-rigged ships, limited in their ability to tack, were driven astern, out of control.

The problems of treacherous winds were compounded by poor visibility. In winter, heavy rain obscured the passage. The annual rainfall off Cape Flattery is 106 inches (2,700 mm), four times Victoria's, just 43 nautical miles to the east. Much of this comes in massive downpours. In summer and fall, the problem was fog. Huge amoeba-like banks of advection fog slunk in and out of Juan de Fuca with deceptive speed. A captain approaching the strait could be contemplating the snowy toque of Sekiu Peak in the Olympic Mountains one minute, and struggling to make out the bow of his ship the next. Under such circumstances, captains would have to navigate by dead reckoning, which took on a literal meaning when the water-slapped rocks of Carmanah Point loomed. The heavy west coast surf surrendered few ships that went aground.

The combined forces of wind and fog delivered up wrecks with remarkable frequency, earning the coast the title "Graveyard of the Pacific." It was not long before ship owners and captains were demanding the assistance of powerful tugs to lead their vessels in and out of West Coast ports. And by powerful they did not mean the aging *Beaver*.

Nor was the situation any better once the ships were safely tucked inside a harbour. Boasts by Vancouver's infant business community that it was a world-class port were undermined by the presence of a variegated collection of watercraft that serviced the big ocean-going vessels. These little craft shunted scow loads of coal or lumber alongside, or assisted with docking. Undoubtedly the strangest of them was the *Union*, an indigenous boat borne of a partnership. One man had a scow, another

A COMBINATION OF WIND, WEATHER AND CURRENTS MADE THE ENTRANCE TO THE JUAN DE FUCA STRAIT TREACHEROUS FOR SQUARE RIGGERS.

a threshing-machine engine. They attached a paddle wheel and went into business. The *Union* had one gear—ahead—hence its more common name, "Sudden Jerk." Stopping was achieved by slowing the engine or, when the throttle cable snapped, as it often did, by stuffing gunny sacks into the chain drives or colliding with something solid, like a piling. A buoy was chained to the engine on the probable odds that the hull would disintegrate.

Among those decrying the woeful state of towboats in the 1880s were James Dunsmuir and his younger brother, Alexander. The two had assumed management of the family coal business from their father, Robert, and were eager to put their own stamp on company affairs. Both James, who ran the operation on Vancouver Island, and Alex, who tended the company office in San Francisco, knew firsthand the trouble sailing ships were having taking company coal from mines in Wellington and Comox to eager customers on the American west coast. The best way to rectify the situation, they concluded, was to have a tug built.

In 1888 the Dunsmuirs chose renowned San Francisco naval architect George Middlemas to design a vessel. The plan Middlemas came up with was, in its essential features, the prototype for the next hundred years of coastal towboats: strong hull, powerful engines, large screw, deep draft. No cabins for passengers, no holds for cargo. The pilothouse was high, for visibility, the aft bulwarks low, so the towline could swing freely. The tow post was mounted low and positioned about a third the distance from stern to bow—the best location for manoeuvrability. Unlike the *Beaver*, it was a single-purpose vessel; Middlemas's tug was designed to tow and nothing else.

To the Dunsmuirs' credit, they had the new tug's hull and engines built locally, rather than at the proven boatyards and machine shops of San Francisco. The contract to build the boat was awarded to Robert Laing, a Scottish boatbuilder who had moved to Victoria in 1850. It was a massive project for a local firm. Drays freighted with lumber and supplies streamed into the yard. The hull was built of select air-dried 5-inch lumber and sheathed with 1,337 sheets of copper.

Within earshot of the boatyard, engineers at Albion Iron Works were busy assembling the boiler and engine. The works were owned by Joseph Spratt, a San Francisco-trained engineer who had built his business powering sternwheelers during the gold rush. Following Middlemas's instructions, Spratt built two massive boilers with a total heating surface of 2,782 square feet. These would provide steam to

VANCOUVER'S REPUTATION AS A WORLD-CLASS PORT WASN'T ENHANCED BY THE PRESENCE OF HOMEMADE CRAFT SUCH AS THE *UNION*, A SCOW POWERED BY A THRESHING MACHINE ENGINE.

two equally monstrous engines, which weighed 25 tons apiece. The engines were so heavy the yard had to construct a special set of shears to lower them into the hull.

It was the most public shipbuilding in BC history. Victorians were kept abreast of the new ship's progress almost daily. There was an air of tension about the project for, as the *Daily Colonist* noted, the vessel was a test of Victoria's shipbuilding industry. If the boat was successful, local shipyards could expect more work; if it failed, future work would continue to go to San Francisco yards. In particular, the success or failure of the engines would prove crucial to the future of the boiler industry. Day after day articles appeared, each attempting to convey the scope of the project: the heft of the main shaft, 9.75 inches in diameter; the bulk of the bilge pump capable of throwing 1,000 gallons a minute. The great cylinders evidenced "the founder's art." A touring journalist, taken with the engine's appointments, wrote: "they are to be covered and finished off with brass bands, forming a very tasty and neat completion." When the papers ran out of engine talk, they could always mention the Dunsmuir brothers.

James and Alex were as different as steam and sail. James, dark and retiring, had inherited his parents' dour view of the world. Alex was verbose, ebullient, a handsome man with reddish sideburns and a quick eye for women. No sooner was he dispatched south to establish an office in San Francisco than he took up with a married actress, Edna Wallace. As a young man in Nanaimo, James passed his days learning about ledgers; Alex was learning lore from a Native named Coal Tyee. Neither brother was particularly liked, though Alex less so, because of his unpleasant habit of asking for things in baby talk. "Snobs," as he was called by intimates, was frequently absent as well, suffering through a hangover in a comfy chair with a pillow between his knees. The differences between the two brothers would find focus in the new boat.

JAMES DUNSMUIR (LEFT), THE ELDER OF TWO BROTHERS, TOOK OVER THE FAMILY BUSINESS, THEN ENTERED POLITICS AND SERVED AS PREMIER OF BC. HIS YOUNGER BROTHER ALEX EVENTUALLY DIED OF ALCOHOLISM.

In June 1889, the *Daily Colonist* reported the Dunsmuir ship, final cost $60,000, was ready to launch, awaiting only "the order of the owners and favorable tide." The Dunsmuirs chose June 3. Alex was determined to make the event a grand occasion, fitting the latest addition to the family's expanding empire. Events, however, conspired to take some of the shimmer off the day. Prior to the launch, the shipbuilders had requested that the government dredger, stationed nearby, clear a deep channel by the ways to ensure a safe launching. The harbour engineer, a man named Gamble, said the job would take a mere two hours, but first he required permission from Ottawa. Infuriated, Alex Dunsmuir and the builders appealed to the local MP, Lt. Col. E.G. Prior, who eventually telegraphed the minister of public works for approval. Approval was given, but not before engineer Gamble had left town on business. When other arrangements were made to get the dredger moved, it was discovered the government tug *Pilot* was preoccupied. Only the *Pilot* was permitted to move the dredger.

Such nonsense may have been okay for society's lower classes, but it would not do for Dunsmuirs. They decided to launch the tug anyway. Never a family to miss a chance to coddle the powers that be, the Dunsmuirs christened their new tug the *Lorne* to honour the Marquess of Lorne, Governor General, whose wife was Princess Louise, fourth daughter of Queen Victoria. The tug slid majestically down the ways, but instead of riding easily into the harbour's waters, it skidded sideways on the bottom. Subsequent investigation revealed the harbour was indeed too shallow; a large area of the hull's copper plating had been ground off. Quick to side with the Dunsmuirs, the newspaper announced the problem was the result of "too much red tape and too little judgement in Victoria officialdom."

By late August the *Lorne*'s housework was complete and the ship was ready for sea trials. One of the last touches was to hang portraits of the Dunsmuirs in the dining room. To command the new ship in its first runs, the brothers chose Captain James Christensen, former pilot and veteran seaman. Christensen was a sturdy man with an honest face weathered like dry firewood. He knew the coast as few others did. Christensen had arrived in BC as a bosun on a Norwegian vessel then jumped ship for work in the local trade. The roster of his commands reads like the all-star list of pioneering West Coast ships: *Surprise, Pilot, Beaver.* Genial at parties, he was fearless at sea and known as the Crazy Dutchman. He pioneered the sealing industry and was involved in the daring apprehension, in 1869, of ten Natives accused in the murder of the crew of the wrecked vessel *John Bright.* Hardworking and flamboyant, Christensen embodied qualities the brothers wanted in the *Lorne.*

TRAINED IN LOCAL WATERS ABOARD THE *BEAVER*, CAPT. JAMES CHRISTENSEN COMMANDED THE *LORNE*, THEN WORKED AS A COASTAL PILOT UNTIL THE AGE OF EIGHTY.

The Dunsmuirs celebrated the completion of the ship with a gala run. Decks crowded with Victoria's elite, it sped out of Esquimalt harbour, ensign snapping at the stern. Crowds of onlookers cheered from shore. Captain Christensen let blast with the ship's whistle, and nearby vessels answered in chorus. A passenger on board wrote: "She ran easily, without the usual pounding of new machinery, and threw the water from her bows like an 'ocean greyhound.'"

Alex Dunsmuir, who had pressed to launch the ship without the dredger, was so elated with the celebrations that he lobbied his business-minded brother to delay putting the ship to work and scheduled another party run. This time the ship carried its cargo of partiers to Race Rocks, where "even in the teeth of a strong breeze, it made 14 knots." Then Alex decided it would be fun to go on an overnight trip. Brother James opposed the idea, but Alex and his baby talk prevailed. This time the destination was Comox. Guests included MP Prior and a member of the provincial legislature. James registered his opposition to the jaunt by refusing to take part, claiming pressing business demands instead. After a tour of the company mines in Comox, the guests enjoyed themselves hunting, fishing and feasting. The tug returned to Victoria, unloaded her cargo of overfed, weary guests and finally was deemed ready for business.

Like all towboats, the hierarchy on the *Lorne* was well defined: master or captain, mate, engineers, firemen, a cook and deckhands. There were thirteen crew in all. As the legal, moral and historical chief of the ship, the captain, or "Old Man," as he was called, usually claimed rights to the best accommodation, though on the *Lorne* this privilege was shared with the Dunsmuirs, who kept one of two well-appointed rooms for themselves. The captain's cabin, fitted in cedar and pine, was immediately behind the wheelhouse.

Firemen and deckhands had little responsibility but lived in poorer conditions. Theirs was a hard physical job. Firemen on the *Lorne* shovelled up to 15 tons of coal a day. When they were not shovelling they cleaned ashes. In winter, when the deckhands were freezing their fingers on the cold rigging and getting hollered at by the Old Man, a fireman could pretend his job was modestly pleasant. The engine room was warm, and the only noise was the hiss of the valves and the scrape of shovel on coal. A good tender could work for ten minutes, then have a cigarette. In summer, however, the pleasures reversed. Even the best firemen worked in a blast-furnace hell, while the deckhands idled away the hours chipping paint in shirt-sleeves.

The unofficial job description of life aboard the *Lorne* was defined by the saying "hurry up and wait." Frantic moments of activity—when coming alongside a ship in heavy seas, for instance—were separated by long periods of boredom. When off watch, crew passed the time reading, talking or ribbing the junior members. A favourite prank was to send a new deckhand on an impossible mission, such as searching for red and green oil to put in the red and green running lights. Another trick was to have a new man take a sounding through a hole in the deck that led to the freshwater tanks. The inevitable discovery that the ship was running in mere feet of water was good for a week's worth of guffaws.

One of the *Lorne*'s first jobs was towing the British ship *Titania* from Esquimalt to Cape Flattery. At Race Rocks, the *Lorne* and its tow were clobbered by a sudden squall. Soon the tow was ploughing through huge seas. Conditions were so bad a nearby ship, the *Wilmington*, was forced to seek shelter in Neah Bay. But Captain Christensen

chose to press on. "A terrific sea was running," he later recalled; "the lightning was blinding and seemed like one sheet of flame constantly enveloping the boat and illuminating the angry water, while the peals of thunder were deafening." Despite heavy seas, the *Lorne* made a steady 8 knots, finally casting the *Titania* free off Cape Flattery. It then took in tow the collier *Yosemite* and delivered it to Departure Bay. Elated with the tug's performance, the ebullient Captain Christensen declared the *Lorne* the "staunchest, handsomest and best handling boat on the Pacific Coast!"

With its great wedge-shaped hull, the *Lorne* was a fine sea boat. But it was never nimble enough to work well in confined harbours. The ship's massive wooden rudder was turned via a block and tackle and huge wooden wheel. It took two strong men spinning this wheel eighteen turns to bring the ship about. Recalling a trip on the *Lorne*, Charles W. Cates, a veteran seaman and towboater whose father founded a pioneer BC towing firm, described how the tug was entering Vancouver harbour near the south shore when the order was given to bring it about. Despite the Herculean efforts of two men at the helm, the ship was unable to complete the turn; it had to go astern before it ran into the opposite shore. The harbour at that point is 2 nautical miles wide.

The *Lorne*'s towline was equally cumbersome. It was a massive hawser, made of the best Manila hemp, 16 inches in circumference and 1,800 feet long. It was usually brought in by a steam capstan. When the weather was rough, as it frequently was when the *Lorne* released an outbound sailing ship off Cape Flattery, the tug's aft decks were unsafe. The *Lorne* then dragged the line for 35 nautical miles, until it reached sheltered waters. Then the crew started the capstan and brought the line in.

Early in the first year of service, the *Lorne* picked up the sailing ship *Glory of the Seas*, bound for Nanaimo. As Captain Christensen altered course to bring both ships into the wind, a squall struck. Instantly, the sails of the ship—the main royals, skysails, and mizzen royals—were blown clear of their bolt ropes. The gusts blew the ship nearly on its beam ends, where it remained, unable to manoeuvre. Aboard the *Lorne*, all the crew could do was cast off the hawser and watch in fascinated horror. For several minutes the fate of the sailing ship was uncertain. Then, as the nimble crew scaled the rigging and cleared away the tattered canvas, the vessel returned to an even keel.

To the Dunsmuirs' delight, the *Lorne* was often taxed to perform all the work required. In a two-week period in December 1897, for example, it towed the collier

A FORMER TEA CLIPPER, THE *TITANIA* WAS BOUGHT BY THE HUDSON'S BAY COMPANY AND PLACED ON THE ENGLAND–VICTORIA RUN.

Eclipse from Departure Bay to Cape Flattery, returning with the bark *Columbia* in ballast to Port Townsend; towed the German bark *Magellanes* into Vancouver; the *Glory of the Seas* from Comox to sea; worked as far south as the Columbia River to fetch the lumber-laden barkentine *Leslie D.*; hauled the ship *America* from Comox and the collier *Rufus E. Wood* from Nanaimo to Cape Flattery. In the same month, the *Lorne* towed the coal-laden, 1,700-ton *Sterling* from Nanaimo to Cape Flattery in thirteen hours, thirty minutes, a record for the day.

When it wasn't towing coal or lumber ships, the *Lorne* often assisted ships of the sealing fleet. Sealers knew it as the fleet mother. Since the tug was the last sight for crews heading on long voyages, occasionally their children would be allowed to ride the *Lorne* as it towed a schooner to sea. It was an immensely emotional time, and children would weep as they watched their fathers sail away on journeys that lasted months. For some children, the sight of a sealing schooner being yanked behind the *Lorne* was the last memory of their fathers.

In the days before ship-to-shore radio, the *Lorne* often received orders via flag signals at the Cape Flattery lighthouse. Otherwise, it freelanced. The captain became business agent, haggling with miserly sailing ship captains over rates. On one occasion the *Lorne* was negotiating with an American four-masted schooner over the fee to tow him in from Cape Flattery. "Take you in to Townsend for $150," the *Lorne*'s captain offered. The schooner captain refused, hoping to get a better deal from a competing tug. What he got instead was a storm, which forced him out to sea for a month. By the time he returned, the *Lorne*'s fee had surged to $250—which he grudgingly accepted. When weather was foul there was little dickering; sailing vessels would take any tow at virtually any price. The *Lorne* would plough through heavy seas to pick up waiting sailing ships. Sometimes these ships had been holding for weeks. In the early 1890s the *Lorne* was running in heavy fog between Cape Flattery and Carmanah Point when it came across a ship lost in the fog and drifting toward the beach. The vessel was out of Liverpool, bound for Burrard Inlet. It had been at sea for 180 days. The crew had survived on hardtack and salted horse meat. For several days they had been on Calashee watch—all hands on deck. They were exhausted and afraid. The *Lorne* took the ship in tow. At Royal Roads, the tug came alongside its tow and a deckhand hollered for the crew to step aboard. In the *Lorne*'s dining

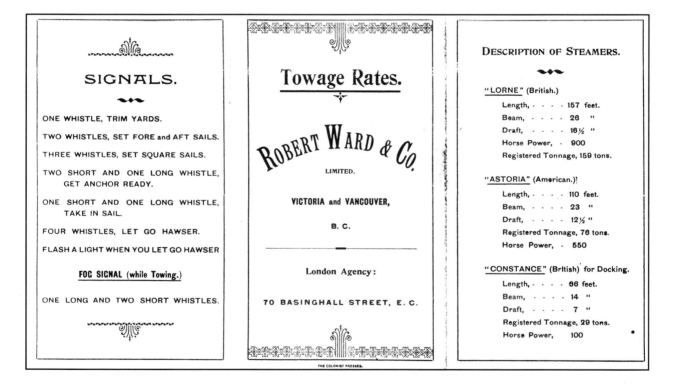

room the hungry sailors found the table groaning with sumptuous roasts, vegetables and fresh bread. One of the young apprentices from the ship who dug into the meal was Barney Johnson. Smart and enterprising, Johnson earned his master's papers, then built up Hecate Straits Towing into a powerful firm whose fleet eventually included the *Lorne*.

In fine weather the *Lorne* couldn't buy a tow. Proud, parsimonious captains thumbed their noses at the towboats and took their vessels right up the strait. If the weather had just broken, there would be a fleet of such ships. All the *Lorne* could do

IN THE DAYS BEFORE MARINE RADIOS, TOWBOATS PASSED OUT RATE CARDS, WHICH INCLUDED SIGNAL INFORMATION, TO VESSELS THEY WERE ABOUT TO TAKE UNDER TOW.

was run alongside and admire the view: the great smacks of sail, the splash of bows in waves, the hollered instructions of seamen. It was a scene that even the most optimistic proponent of sail knew would soon be memory.

Fierce competition for towing work often pitted American outfits against their Canadian counterparts. In 1898 the *Lorne* was called upon to tow the steamer *Corona* from a Lewis Island reef. The tow was proceeding past Entrance Island when the warship USS *Percy* arrived. The *Lorne*'s crew watched as the navy boat came alongside the *Corona* and some papers were hurriedly exchanged. The *Percy* then took a position astern. A short while later the American tug *Pioneer* joined the procession. Then, without warning, the *Corona* released the *Lorne*'s towline, and the *Pioneer* escorted the steamer to Port Townsend. The *Lorne*'s owners and the Victoria press were outraged at the US government-sanctioned breach of conduct. On the south shore of Juan de Fuca, American newspapers were equally vociferous in their defence of the action, which, they darkly hinted, had to do with secret treasury department dealings. They erroneously reported the *Percy* had threatened to fire a shot across the *Lorne*'s bows unless it halted. After journalistic volleys back and forth, the mundane truth eventually emerged; the *Corona*'s captain was afraid of arriving in Victoria lest he be sued under British law by the *Corona*'s passengers for damages in the wreck. The *Colonist* concluded the affair with a rare (albeit ungrammatical) bit of wisdom. "All men are liars," wrote the editors, "more especially the fellow [newspapermen] over at Port Townsend."

THREE OF THE *LORNE*'S CREW POSE WHILE AT SWANSON BAY, SITE OF ONE OF THE FIRST PULP MILLS IN BC.

Traditionally, seamen on coastal boats are less superstitious than their ocean-going brethren. Portents of trouble—a bouquet of forget-me-nots, a black handbag, the loss of a bucket overboard—that send a deep-sea man sprinting for a newborn's caul (a remedy for ill luck) are laughable to the shore-based seaman. Until they ran into a notorious black cat, the crew of the *Lorne* shared this skepticism. In 1906 the *Lorne* was standing by in the west entrance to Juan de Fuca Strait, waiting for a chance to tow a sailing ship. Off Barkley Sound, on a clear day, an alert crewman spotted masts in the distance. The *Lorne* went to investigate. The schooner appeared to be in distress so a man was put aboard. The vessel, inexplicably, was derelict. Scrambling through the galley and officers' quarters, the man from the *Lorne* was astonished to find the ship was empty—except for a scrawny black cat. The cat was cowering near a sea chest. He scooped up the cat and headed across the deserted decks for the tug. On the way, he slipped and broke his leg. The tug, in

attempting to come alongside, crashed into the schooner and smashed several timbers. Some of the crew suggested throwing the cat overboard with a boom chain for a life vest, but the captain refused.

When the *Lorne* returned to Vancouver it went ahead instead of astern and crashed into the wharf. There was a dispute between labour and management, and the crew walked off.

Somehow, Charles W. Cates's uncle, Captain Jim Cates, was elected to look after the cat. Through his marine connections he traced the cat's owners in San Francisco. He put the animal in a box and passed the box onto the next ship bound for that city. On the way south the ship ran aground. Eventually it made its way to San Francisco. The cat was put on the wharf on April 18—at the very moment the San Francisco earthquake struck. The crew of the *Lorne* got news of the disaster from the lighthouse keeper at Neah Bay, who used to convey news and weather reports to passing ships by megaphone. "Black cat delivered safely at San Francisco," he reported. "City completely destroyed by earthquake and fire."

In 1903 the Dunsmuirs sold the *Lorne*. It floated through a number of owners including the Grand Trunk Pacific (towing rail barges), Hecate Straits Towing and, finally, Pacific (Coyle) Navigation Company, where it towed giant Davis rafts (floating bundles of logs) containing more than a million board feet of timber.

As one of the most powerful tugs on the West Coast, the *Lorne* was regularly called upon for salvage work. In 1890, the tug received word the *Highland Light* was foundering near Hand Island in Barkley Sound and towed her, leaking badly, to

Esquimalt. In 1907 the *Alice Gertrude* foundered on Clallan Reef and was knocked to pieces. The *Lorne*, along with the *Wyadda*, helped remove passengers and crew. In 1911 the *William Jolliffe* and the *Lorne* pulled the *Tees* from a beach in Barkley Sound. The *Tees* was later refitted as the Pacific Salvage tug *Salvage Queen*.

The *Lorne* was not immune to mishap, either. In August 1914 the tug was towing the barge *America* when both vessels went aground in Kanaka Bay, San Juan Island. Both were salvaged; the *Lorne* was towed to Victoria for repairs. On another occasion the *Lorne* was towing the log barge *Pacific Gatherer* under the Second Narrows rail bridge. The tow was caught in an eddy and the barge sheered under the bridge's centre span. It stuck fast, held tight by current and rising tide. For an hour, the *Lorne*'s master, Captain Barney Johnson, and the crew watched as the barge heaved the 8,000-ton span off its mounts, like a weightlifter shouldering a record lift. Then the

FOG WAS BLAMED FOR THE GROUNDING OF THE *LORNE* AND THE BARGE *AMERICA* IN AUGUST 1914.

bridge tumbled into the narrows. "It was the biggest damn splash anybody has ever seen," said Captain Johnson.

The details of the *Lorne*'s fate are uncertain. In 1936, her useful days over, the *Lorne* was tied up at Terminal Dock. At low tide the ship went aground, then keeled over. A valve had thoughtlessly been left open and the ship flooded. Most likely it was bought by the Shaeffer-Haggert company and dismantled at the BC Marine Engineers and Shipbuilders Yard. Sentimental mariners, though, prefer to think its remains lie off Gambier Island in Howe Sound, where the BC towboat fleet the *Lorne* pioneered continues to run.

(TOP) BARNEY JOHNSON FIRST SAW THE *LORNE* FROM THE DECK OF A SAILING SHIP APPROACHING THE COAST. HE LATER BOUGHT THE TUG AND SKIPPERED IT FOR MANY YEARS.

(BOTTOM) "[T]HE BIGGEST DAMN SPLASH ANYBODY HAS EVER SEEN," SAID THE *LORNE*'S CAPTAIN WHEN THE TUG'S BARGE, THE *PACIFIC GATHERER*, DISLODGED THE SECOND NARROWS RAIL BRIDGE IN BURRARD INLET.

Thermopylae

O f all the sailing ships working the seas in the late 1800s, only a half dozen were so fine, so swift and handsome, that grocers and washerwomen could reel off their names as readily as seamen. One of these ships was the *Thermopylae*. Built to compete in the elite China-to-England tea trade, the *Thermopylae* demolished most significant speed records of the day. For three decades its great spans of sail, slung from masts towering fifteen stories above the sleek green hull, were common sights on the Pacific, Atlantic and Indian oceans. Such was the great ship's renown that sailors throughout the world considered it an honour to be passed by the *Thermopylae*.

TEA CLIPPERS GATHERED AT A LOADING SITE NEAR FOOCHOW, CHINA TO COLLECT THE TEA HARVEST, AND THE CREW OF THE FIRST ONE BACK TO ENGLAND ENJOYED THE BEST PROFITS. AS A "FULL-BLOOD" CLIPPER, THE *THERMOPYLAE* WAS ONE OF THE FIRST SHIPS TO LOAD AND GET AWAY.

From 1891 to 1896 the *Thermopylae* called Victoria home port. It was beyond prime, its rigging worn, its weathered hull extruding oakum caulking. But British Columbians welcomed it with an enthusiasm usually reserved for a vessel just off the shipbuilder's ways. Desperate for an Old World history, settlers had already scrawled the names of lochs and lords across the face of the new land. To complete the reinvention of the coast they needed a European-style maritime tradition. There were the *Discovery* and the *Beaver*, but they were important only in the context of the Northwest. What the colonists needed was a truly great ship, one that would do for the new province what a knighted ancestor does to a humble family: give it a legacy. In the aging ship they found their answer. For above all, the *Thermopylae* was a ship with a history.

The *Thermopylae* was built in 1868 in Aberdeen, Scotland. Sprawled around the fingering arms of the rivers Don and Dee, the Aberdeen shipyards were rivalled only by Clyde-based yards as producers of the fastest ships in the British Isles. The type of ships they built were called clippers, because they "clipped" speed off the times of the previously swiftest vessels, the so-called packets. Clipper ships were marked by long, slim hulls, enormous amounts of sail and extended bowsprits. Fast, temperamental and expensive, they were built exclusively to haul tea from China to London.

The tea trade, as it was called, was one of the costliest but potentially most rewarding ventures of the time. Each June, British clippers mustered at the mouth of the Min River, near Foochow, China, to await arrival of the year's tea crop. When the harvest was ready it was brought down the river in sampans. As soon as a ship was loaded it set for England. The first ship back earned its sponsoring merchant a huge profit. To encourage swift passages, captain and crew of the first ship were rewarded with a one-pound-per-ton bonus and the right to mount a golden cock from the mainmast, signaling the ship was the "cock of the walk."

The rush to return to London led to some of the greatest sailing races of all time. In 1866, for example, five clippers left Foochow within thirty-six hours of each other. After ninety-nine days of flawless sailing, the *Taeping* arrived at the London Docks at 9:45 p.m., September 6. It was followed by the *Ariel* at 10:15 p.m. and the *Serica* at 11:30 p.m. The three vessels were so close they went up the Thames on the same tide. The other two ships, the *Fiery Cross* and the *Taitsing* arrived two days later. All five vessels travelled 14,000 nautical miles.

THE *THERMOPYLAE*'S FINE LINES ARE EVIDENT IN THIS VIEW OF THE STERN, 1895, AT BULLEN'S WAY (LATER YARROWS) IN ESQUIMALT.

During the 1860s, Clyde-built clippers held dominion in the tea trade. But in 1868 the owner of the Aberdeen White Star Line, George Thompson, decided to challenge the Clyde's supremacy. He commissioned marine engineer Bernard Waymouth to design a vessel expressly to win the races. An unimposing, compact figure with cold appraising eyes, Waymouth was an expert in the emerging field of composite shipbuilding—a technique that married iron and wood in hulls. Waymouth had first become captivated by the clipper designs when, as a young apprentice ambling the London waterfront in 1851, he spotted the sleek American vessel *Oriental*. The *Oriental*, based on a design pioneered by the revolutionary Nova Scotia-born shipbuilder Donald Mackay, had just arrived from Hong Kong in the unheard-of time of ninety-seven days. It was one of the first foreign ships allowed into England after the repeal of the British Navigation Laws, and it showed how far behind British shipbuilders had fallen.

Standing amid the crowds of interested onlookers, Waymouth pulled a notebook from his breast pocket and sketched the American ship's salient lines: the sweep of the stern, the long, graceful bow. In coming years, these drawings would be Waymouth's source for several ships. Among them was the *Leander*, launched in 1867. A swift, quick-tempered ship, the *Leander* had impressed seamen with its ability to run well on a slight breeze, but was kept from reaching its full potential, it was widely thought, because of the owner's insistence on keeping an inept master at the helm.

In the *Thermopylae* Waymouth incorporated his most radical ideas. Sacrificing cargo space for speed, he designed the vessel with finely pointed bow and stern. An unusual feature of the hull was that its widest point was 3 feet under the waterline, instead of at the waterline, as was the case with most clippers. Combined with a large tumblehome—or inward flare of the hull above the widest point—the ship was designed to ride well when keeled over. For sail, Waymouth chose width over height. Demastings were becoming common on ships with high masts; his alternative called

NINETY-NINE DAYS AND 14,000 NAUTICAL MILES AFTER LEAVING FOOCHOW, THE CLIPPERS *TAEPING* AND *ARIEL* WERE STILL ABEAM AND RACING UP THE ENGLISH CHANNEL.

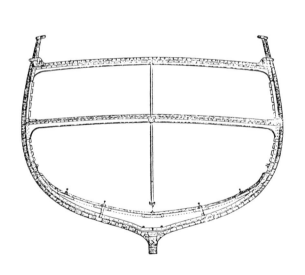

for longer yards. The *Thermopylae*'s great main yard was 80 feet long and supported a sail 40 feet deep—larger than a tennis court. When all canvas was spread, the *Thermopylae* boasted 32,000 square feet—almost a full acre.

During the summer of 1868, Waymouth watched his idea take form in the builders' yard. Scottish shipwrights, like the craft they were building, were a special breed. Part technician, part artisan, they signalled their pride by wearing top hats to work. They picked over the shipyard's lumber stacks like chefs at a fruit stand, eyeing each timber for warp and grain, rejecting this piece, accepting that. The result was that every plank and beam of elm, oak and teak used in the hull was flawless. Fastened to iron ribs, then sheathed in Muntz metal, a copper-like compound, the hull warranted a Lloyd's rating of 17A1, meaning it was guaranteed sound and safe for at least seventeen years. The shipwrights, too, had their own test for the new vessel. When the hull was launched, on August 19, they rode it from the ways into the harbour. Then, along with all the hands in the yard, they ran in a gang from side to side to test the stability. They also pronounced the ship fit for sea.

Like many shipbuilders of the day, Thompson was partial to classical names for new vessels. He chose *Thermopylae*, location of the heroic Spartan battle against the Persians in 480 BC. Its figurehead was King Leonidas of Sparta, helmeted, shield held aloft in one hand, a sword clutched in the other. (The sword was removable; it was unsheathed upon arrival in port, and sheathed on departure.)

To command his new ship, Thompson chose Captain Robert Kemball, a heavyset man with a towering forehead, deep, slightly quizzical eyes and a beard that, one suspects, hid a massively undersized chin. Kemball's previous commands included the *Yangtze*, from whose unremarkable hull he had coaxed some fine runs. He had also endeared himself to the sailing fraternity with his feats of navigation, such as traversing the Flores Sea's treacherous Atlas Strait in moonlight, an accomplishment that may be compared to jogging a winding cliffside footpath while blindfolded. Assisting Kemball was the chief mate, Charles Matheson, a veteran of the *Colonial Empire* and a steady seaman. One carpenter, a cook, various officers and twenty-two able seamen rounded out the complement to thirty-six.

For the *Thermopylae*'s first trip, Kemball chose to follow the traditional route to China. The route had three legs. After leaving London it headed south along the west

(TOP) THE FINE LINES OF THE AMERICAN SHIP *ORIENTAL* WERE THE INSPIRATION FOR BERNARD WAYMOUTH'S CLIPPER DESIGNS.

(BOTTOM) A CROSS-SECTION OF THE *THERMOPYLAE*'S HULL, ONCE SAID TO RESEMBLE THE PROFILE OF AN AUSTRALIAN GUM NUT.

coast of Africa, then across the Atlantic to the east coast of Brazil. Off Argentina it caught the west winds sweeping along the fortieth parallel called the "Roaring Forties." The winds sped the ships onward around the Cape of Good Hope to Australia, where domestic goods and machinery were traded for coal. The coal went to Singapore or Shanghai, and the vessels carried on to Foochow.

The first trip of any ship is generally uneventful. It's a time when officers and crew literally "learn the ropes." But quickly the *Thermopylae* proved an excellent sailer. Even in a light breeze the ship made 7 knots. In stronger winds it surged to 16, 17, even 18 knots. The harder it was pressed, the further it keeled, until the lee scuppers disappeared in a froth and a man moving about on deck had to hang onto a railing or risk sliding overboard. The hull flexed in heavy seas, too, and as the men soon discovered, the planking had a habit of nipping them as they lay in their bunks. Working in his chart room, Kemball realized the vessel was making over 260 nautical miles in twenty-four hours. He ordered more sail on. There would be no breaking-in period for the ship. They would learn the ropes on the fly.

The *Thermopylae* arrived in Melbourne in sixty-two days, beating the previous record of sixty-five days, set by Donald Mackay's *James Baines* in 1854–55. The run was so phenomenal that the Australian press swarmed the ship, crawling from stem to gudgeon in search of its secrets. "The fastest and handsomest ship in the world is now lying at the Circular Quay," declared one paper. Their reports, while informative, also suggest the average newspaper reader then was as conversant with nautical terms as the average late-twentieth-century newspaper reader is with computer terms.

"Cunningham's patent forebrace machine is used in swinging the foreyard."

"The length of the jibboom from the knight heads to the flying jibboom end is over eighty feet."

"She has two swinging booms fifty feet in length, her lower studding sails having twenty-two clothes in the head."

From Melbourne, the *Thermopylae* sailed light to Newcastle, New South Wales, where it loaded bagged coal bound for Shanghai. The Newcastle–Shanghai run usually took forty-five to fifty-five days. The *Thermopylae* was dockside in Shanghai in twenty-eight days—setting another record. Captain Kemball was elated. The ship had already set two records and it hadn't even begun to race.

From Shanghai it was a short hop to Foochow. To celebrate their arrival Kemball fired one of the two cannons on board (they were there to defend against pirates), and a brazen crewman scaled the rigging and attached a golden cock to the mainmast.

At Foochow, crews of waiting clippers, many Clyde-built, greeted news of the *Thermopylae*'s accomplishments with incredulity. The Aberdeen vessel, they said, was lucky on its passage to Australia and caught a freak slant, or favourable wind, on the journey to Shanghai. They called the ship "old dromedary," or "that damned Scotsman." They were especially irked by Kemball's boasting, which he did magnificently,

CAPT. ROBERT KEMBALL, FAMOUS FOR HIS NAUTICAL ACHIEVEMENTS, COMMANDER OF THE *THERMOPYLAE*.

JAMES BAINES.

dressed in pale pongee silk while reclining on deck under the shade of white awnings. Night after night, sailors on other clippers listened to Kemball's sonorous trumpeting drift across the anchorage—how the *Thermopylae* surged in the slightest breeze, how it ran like a greyhound. One of Kemball's favourite expressions was that the *Thermopylae* could "make seven knots in a breeze that wouldn't blow out a candle." Aboard the *Thermopylae*, briny water gave way to tea; hardtack to cucumber sandwiches. The growly old salt had miraculously transformed into a classic British "dink in a pith helmet."

The bluster was too much for seamen on the other clippers. Records or no records, the new ship had its place. Fights between crews erupted in local drinking establishments. One night a sailor from a nearby ship (likely the *Taeping*) slipped into the dirty, dun-coloured waters of the Min, scaled the *Thermopylae*'s rigging and stripped the golden cock from the mast. Even residents of the nearby tweedy British colony did not appreciate the boastful nature of the *Thermopylae*'s arrival. In a letter to the *Shanghai Evening Courier*, a local claimed the cannon shot had caused his mount to rear, tossing him headlong into the river. From all directions the harrumphing about the *Thermopylae* was audible.

The sampans arrived in late June 1869. They drifted down the river like a fleet of oversized waterbugs. Suddenly, idling and crowing was replaced with industry. Though there were forty ships in the tea fleet, only the "full bloods" loaded first. It was a laborious process; from the sampans the chests of tea, weighing 65 pounds each, were hoisted aboard then lowered into the hold. In the hold the chests were stowed with an eye to weight and safety. The *Thermopylae* was so finely built that an inch difference in fore-and-aft trim affected its speed by a knot or more. To help pass the time, the crew chanted shanties:

Hi, Hi, Hi, Ching, Ching, Ching, Chinaman, son of a gun, me no likee him!

The Chinese, it is recorded, responded in kind.

Though the *Thermopylae*'s mate drove the crew hard, several ships beat it out of harbour. The first was the *Ariel*, a strong and lively Clyde-built ship that always showed well. The *Ariel* was followed the next day by the *Lahloo*, the *Leander* and, on the third day, the *Spindrift*. Finally, on July 3, the *Thermopylae*, loaded with over a million pounds of prime "first chop" tea, set sail. The race was on.

DONALD MACKAY'S FINE SHIP, THE *JAMES BAINES*, WHOSE LONG-HELD RECORD WAS DEMOLISHED BY THE *THERMOPYLAE* ON ITS FIRST VOYAGE.

Off the coast of China, the *Leander*, winner of the previous year's race by a stunning eighteen-day margin, soon passed the *Ariel* and the *Lahloo*. With the southwest monsoons in full force, it beat down the China Sea in eighteen days, such a good start, the crew believed, that it would be unbeatable. But several days later a passing steamer, the *Achilles*, also out from China, signalled the *Leander* that the *Thermopylae* had cleared the China Sea in sixteen days and was closing. Two days later the crew of the *Leander* spotted a sail astern. By noon the next day the two vessels were running abeam. As the *Thermopylae* surged past, its crew gave the *Leander* three cheeky cheers. Despite the insult, the crew of the *Leander* could not help but gaze in stupefaction at the *Thermopylae*. M.J. Knight, an officer on the *Leander*, afterwards reflected: "How we looked to her I do not know, but she was the most magnificent picture of a ship under sail that ever I have seen, with her tall spars and great spread of canvas...she swept past us with the full weight of S.E. trader-wind on her quarter. She truly 'walked the waters like a thing of life.'" The *Thermopylae*, Knight calculated, was doing no less than 270 nautical miles a day, while the *Leander* was making a steady 260 nautical miles per day. Twenty-four hours later and the *Thermopylae* was a fleck on the horizon. Knight claimed no other vessel ever passed the *Leander*.

Aboard the *Thermopylae* the crew became obsessed with pressing the ship ever faster. There is a story, perhaps apocryphal, that in an effort to speed the ship on some sailors strung blankets on deck. Awed by the mass of canvas, they clung to the

THE *THERMOPYLAE* LOADING TEA AT FOOCHOW. THE SHIP WAS SO FINELY BUILT THAT A DIFFERENCE OF ONE INCH IN TRIM FORE AND AFT COULD MAKE OR MAR A VOYAGE.

handrails, imbibing the sound of the straining rigging, the quick slosh of water on hull. They knew they were on a great ship, not just a lucky ship. Gold pocket watch in hand, Captain Kemball would give the order to put the ship about. The crew swarmed into the rigging, trimmed the yards, coiled ropes, hauled bowlines and descended—all in less than ten minutes. Arriving off the coast of England the ship hove to to take on a pilot. For the first time in almost three months the decks were level. Captain Kemball collared the pilot as he climbed aboard. "Look at that rail," he said, pointing a stubby finger at the hardwood rail. "It is the first time we have seen it since we left China."

The *Thermopylae* arrived at the London Docks in ninety-one days, setting another record. Captain Kemball and his crew dined on champagne for a week. Though the *Sir Lancelot* later shaved two days off the journey, the *Thermopylae* was the only ship to set three records in a single round trip. The passage from Australia to China was never bested by another clipper. The *Thermopylae* was now cock of the walk and legitimately flew the golden rooster, adorned with a streamer of blue bunting.

The *Thermopylae* continued for several years to haul tea, but larger forces had put an end to the races. In 1870 the Suez Canal opened, linking the Red Sea with the Mediterranean. With the Cape of Good Hope cut from the Orient-to-London journey, it was faster to send tea by steamer. Between 1869 and 1878, tea cargo prices dropped from five pounds a ton to three pounds six shillings. More incremental, but equally important, were changes in steamship technology. The advent of the triple-expansion engine, in particular, meant steamers could travel farther, faster and use less coal. With the black smoky signature of the steamship appearing on every sea, even the most committed sailor knew it was only a matter of time before great ships such as the *Thermopylae* were memory.

THE BRITISH CLIPPER *LAHLOO*, BUILT FOR SPEED RATHER THAN CARGO CAPACITY. CLIPPERS HAVE BEEN CALLED "YACHTS IN DISGUISE."

Like many clippers in the post-tea-trade years, the *Thermopylae* found a second career running between Britain and Australia. In London, the ship loaded with all the sundries a colony might expect to need. A cargo list from the 1870s includes 100 boxes of tin plates, 57 packages of books, 18 packages of perfumery, 10 cases of Netherlands spirits, 3 cases of almonds, 4 chests of licorice, 1 hogshead of gelatin, 100 packages of beer, 575 packages of oilstones, 28 marble slabs, 37 cases of bedsteads and 74 packages of medicine.

In Australia the *Thermopylae* loaded wool for England's textile mills. Under Kendall, and later Charles Matheson, who took over command, the ship continued to set fast passage times. During one run, in 1875, it made 303 nautical miles in twenty-four hours. (Vancouver's *Discovery*, by comparison, registered a top daily run of 155 nautical miles.)

Life aboard the *Thermopylae* was hard, but never comparable to the harsh conditions in the *Discovery*. Good sailors, the White Star Line knew, were attracted to good ships. Hence conditions in the forecastle were clean and spacious. The captain's cabin, befitting his position, was lined with teak and lit with shining brass lamps. Off to one side was a well-appointed bathroom and water closet, and to another the saloon and chart room. An officer introduced a black cat to the ship and, unlike the black cat that had scared the crew of the *Lorne*, it quickly became a mascot, snoozing on the decks or licking morsels off the galley floor.

As a flagship the *Thermopylae* was kept in top shape. It took four men

twelve hours to polish all the brass. The pine decks were holystoned so often the wood was bone white. And then there was the rigging. More than 165 separate lines, miles of rope: halyards, braces, tackles, downhauls, clew lines, bowlines, buntlines, lifts, foresail tacks, topsail tacks, gantlines, gaskets and strops. Each had its location, its manner of making fast, and its unique coil, so it would run free though the deck be awash.

The *Thermopylae* had one serious challenger. That was the *Cutty Sark*, a ship of nearly identical dimensions, designed by the renowned Hercules Linton. The two ships met once. In 1872 the *Cutty Sark* and the *Thermopylae* were racing in the Indian Ocean, both bound for England. For days they sailed side by side, the captains wringing every ounce of power from the wind. Then, in heavy seas, the *Cutty Sark* lost its rudder. The *Thermopylae* sailed away to a meaningless victory. Statistically minded marine historians have laboured to extrapolate the race's outcome from logbooks and hull ratios. The *Thermopylae*, they concluded, was likely a better ship in light to moderate winds, the *Cutty Sark* faster in heavy winds. But to seamen, who consider speed an aspect of a ship's worth, not its sum, the argument was debasing. The *Cutty Sark* may have been as fast as the *Thermopylae*, but no ship was faster.

In 1890 the Aberdeen White Star Line sold the *Thermopylae* for £5,000 to William Ross of the Victoria Rice Mill, and Ross later sold it to Robert Reford of Montreal. Reford had noted the rising numbers of Chinese settling in BC and concluded they would be in need of rice. What better way to transport rice, which rots quickly, than in one of the swiftest ships afloat?

In Victoria, news of the purchase thrilled the waterfront. The *Thermopylae*? In BC? Children and adults alike knew the ship's statistics like they would later know the

THE TWO GREAT CLIPPERS *THERMOPYLAE* AND *CUTTY SARK* RACED JUST ONCE. THE RESULT WAS INCONCLUSIVE, AND THE DEBATE CONTINUES ON WHAT THE OUTCOME MIGHT HAVE BEEN HAD THE *CUTTY SARK* NOT LOST ITS RUDDER DURING THE COMPETITION.

point scores for sports stars. The *Daily Colonist* of April 4, 1890, boasted the vessel would bring honour to the young city because it was "said to be one of the fastest, if not the fastest, sailors afloat." Then the paper reprinted, in full, a glowing recount of the *Thermopylae*'s triumphs, taken verbatim from the magazine *London Fairplay* (in colonial BC, British papers were the last word on every subject).

What Victorians could not know, however, was that the superstar was badly aging. The great ship had logged over two decades of hard sailing. Reford was also unfortunate in that his purchase coincided with the tenure of the *Thermopylae*'s only two inept skippers. The first, a Captain Jenkins, took over the ship while it was in Asia. He hawked the lifeboats, studdingsail gear and even one of the muskets from the armoury. Reford replaced him with the mate, twenty-two-year-old John Wilson, who spent the passage across the Pacific drinking.

With all the hype, it was inevitable that the ship would be somewhat of a disappointment—even in top shape. But Victorians could in no way have been prepared for the sad, tattered vessel that entered the harbour one June day in 1891. The rigging was torn, the hull stained. The ship had made an unremarkable journey. The crew blamed Wilson, Wilson blamed the crew. To support his accusations, Wilson offered up his log to a local reporter, who excerpted the juicy bits:

> A.B. was this day beastly drunk, and incapable of doing any work...
> All hands were this day called aft, and in the presence of the steward, each man took lime juice...
> A.B. has fits, and I am feeding him the medicine prescribed.

In the harbour, things went from bad to awful. Traditionally, the best ships attracted the best crews, and in the *Thermopylae*'s heyday, its rigging boasted the classic seamen, whose "every hair was a spun yarn, every finger a marlin spike." The scabrous crowd of toothless wretches that crawled out of the forecastle seemed hardly able to scale a flight of stairs, yet alone the monkey shrouds. Furthermore, when they finally found their land legs, they had a famous blowout in Victoria's hotels. News of their troublemaking preceded them to the ship, and when they stepped aboard, Wilson and the first mate set upon them with belaying pins. The seamen protested to Reford and he fired Wilson and the mate. Suddenly remorseful, the crew pitched in and bought the pair tickets to San Francisco. But now it was Wilson and his mate who kicked up the town. They sold the tickets and invested in fine scotch. Reford fired the worst of the crew, but no ship in port would have them. The reprobate sailors were eventually returned to England under provisions of the appropriately named Distressed British Seamen Act.

Now the owner of an aging purebred with no crew, Reford undertook to make some changes to the *Thermopylae*. He altered the rigging and hired the crew of a well-respected sealing schooner, the *Black Diamond*, which had been seized off the Pribilof Islands by Russians. These "herring-backs," as they were called, were led by Captain Winchester, a forty-four-year-old from Digby, Nova Scotia. From the local docks

Winchester bolstered the crew with several apprentices, including thirteen-year-old Frank Webb. Webb, whose father was a horticulturist who helped design Beacon Hill Park, had dreamed of going to sea. The chance to sail on a legendary ship was not to be turned down.

Under Winchester, the *Thermopylae* regained its legs. On one trip it crossed the Pacific in twenty-nine days. On another, journeying from Yokohama to Victoria, it kept abreast with the swift Canadian Pacific Railway steamer *Empress of India*, logging a steady 16 knots for three days. These crossings, while lacking the thrill of the tea races, often tested the aging ship with terrible weather. On December 14, 1891, the *Thermopylae* departed Nagasaki, bound for Victoria with a load of rice. On

board were a crew of fifteen, less than half the complement the ship had sailed with in the tea trade. In the China Sea it ran into a storm that lasted fifty days. "You can form some idea of the weather we encountered," Captain Winchester later said, "when I tell you that in ten days we only made one mile headway—beating about the whole time." Matters did not improve when the *Thermopylae* reached the Pacific. Hurricane after hurricane pounded the ship, shredding the topsails and badly ripping others. Massive seas washed the decks from stem to stern. The bulwarks caved in. It was freakish weather— in one day the ship sailed past four waterspouts. Something had to give. Finally, a hurricane strained the mizzenmast, rendering it useless. Dirty and exhausted, the crew finally spotted Cape Flattery light. But the ordeal was far from over. For two weeks filthy weather and contrary winds prevented the ship from entering Juan de Fuca Strait. While waiting, the crew ate the last of the stores. Faced with starvation or breaking into the hold, they chose the latter. For the final ten days they lived on rice, cooked in every conceivable manner.

The ship arrived in Victoria a shambles—again. It had been at sea for one hundred days. While the crew hurriedly scrambled ashore to fetch fresh groceries, the captain calculated the damage. Mizzenmast strained, railings gone, bulwarks smashed. Most remarkable was the damage to the sails. The *Thermopylae* had left Bangkok with three complete suits of canvas; it reached Victoria without a presentable or serviceable sail. The trip that should have covered approximately 9,000 nautical miles, Captain Winchester calculated, had traversed almost 15,000 nautical miles.

FLYING CANADIAN COLOURS, THE *THERMOPYLAE* SETS SAIL OFF THE MOUTH OF THE COLUMBIA RIVER. THE FIGURE SCRAMBLING OVER THE SIDE IS A COAST PILOT.

The voyage ended young Webb's sailing career, too. Between seasickness and floggings, he decided to look for adventure elsewhere. According to the family, when the *Thermopylae* docked in Victoria, Webb "took off for the wilds of Saanich."

On the seven trips the *Thermopylae* made while under Canadian registry, all the inbound cargoes were rice. The outbound freights were coal or lumber. To load lumber—shipped as enormous cants, as large as 2 feet square and 100 feet long—hatches were cut in the bow. The ship loaded at the Hastings Mill in Burrard Inlet or the Brunette plant at Sapperton on the Fraser River. Berthed alongside last-leg square-riggers, surrounded by aging sternwheelers, the *Thermopylae* was a Broadway actress reduced to bit pieces in small-town theatricals. In 1895 the *Thermopylae* loaded bulk lumber at Port Blakely, Washington. After a passage of 141 days it arrived at Leith, in Scotland, where it was sold to the Portuguese government for $9,000.

Renamed *Pedro Nunes*, the ship was used as a training ship. It soon became too costly to maintain, and in 1897 it was converted to a coal hulk. Even Clyde ship-builders could not have planned a worse fate. It was often towed alongside the very steamers that had wiped the great sailing ships from the seas. Mercifully, the old

ITS HULL PAINTED WHITE AND CARVED WITH HATCHES TO ACCOMMODATE THE LOADING OF MASSIVE TIMBERS, THE *THERMOPYLAE* TOOK ON LUMBER AT SAPPERTON.

hull's career as a barge was short. On October 13, 1907, in a ceremony acknowledging its storied past, it was towed from the Tagus River and torpedoed.

It is possible to consider the *Thermopylae*'s tenure with Victoria as a mere layover of an aging ship past its prime. Worse still is the thought that its celebration was yet another genuflection of provincial attitude to things British. But that's not how Victorians chose to see it. Just like J.P. Knight, the officer on the *Leander*, Victorians considered it an honour to have the *Thermopylae* pass by. A knot of old mariners dedicated to the preservation of sailing tales united and called themselves the Thermopylae Club. The ship's "fine pedigree"—along with James Douglas's "bold demeanour" and the Fraser River's "rich treasure" of gold—was a mainstay of early published histories. In a eulogy to the vessel written years after its demise and printed in a Victoria newspaper, a former mariner recalled an incident early in the *Thermopylae*'s career that captured the relationship between clipper and town. The great ship had just cleared Port Philip Heads, in Australia. In the distance was the sailing ship HMS *Charybdis*. Both vessels crowded on sail, but as soon as the *Thermopylae* had its mass of canvas set it drew away from the warship. When the captain of the *Charybdis* saw he was outclassed, he flagged the *Thermopylae* in mercantile code. "Goodbye," he signalled. "You are too much for us. It does my heart good to look at you."

THE *THERMOPYLAE* IN ITS LATER INCARNATION AS THE *PEDRO NUNES*, OFF THE COAST OF PORTUGAL.

Beatrice

And since our women must walk Gay
And Money buys their gear,
The Sealing boats must go that way
And filch at hazard year by year.

—Rudyard Kipling

*I*f, as is often alleged, life was slower in the old days, then how did so much get done? In the time it takes a modern urban planner to conceptualize a shopping mall, pioneers built, lived in and abandoned whole towns. Plodding horses, hand-wrung laundry and the slow slap of sail on a windless day may be the ascendant images of the late nineteenth century, but when they saw opportunity, the province's colonists moved at rip speed.

SEALER, TOWBOAT, FREIGHTER, FISH PACKER, MARITIME
RESEARCH PLATFORM—THE *BEATRICE* WORKED THE BC COAST
FOR MORE THAN A CENTURY.

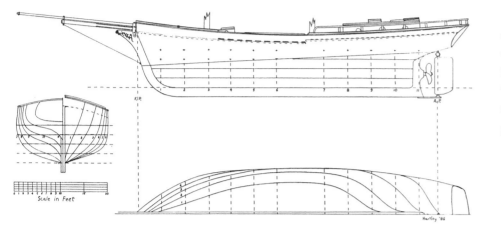

Scale in Feet

Hartley '86

This ability to turn chance to account was especially well developed in the marine industry of the late nineteenth century. Shipbuilders had two great advantages over their modern counterparts (three, if you count gumption). One was easy money. A man wanting to build a ship simply marched into the smoky, red-velvet lounge of Vancouver's Alexandra Hotel, where the wealthy seamen marshalled, and made a pitch. If his idea was sound, he walked away with the cash in his pocket. The other great benefit was lack of regulation. Shipyards were more a matter of attitude than zoning, and certainly unfettered by environmental rules. A shipwright staked out an area above the high tide line, purchased or pinched a few logs and set to work.

It was this ability to wed capital and enterprise that helped BC seafarers cash in on the great pelagic seal hunt. Sealing was to the 1890s what the gold rush was to the 1860s—a free-for-all pitting men against the elements in pursuit of fortune. The hunt set country against country, made and ruined many men and established Victoria as a major Pacific port. Like the gold rush, it was a pivot in history, anchoring BC in the Dominion of Canada at a time when America was contemplating annexing the West Coast from Washington to Alaska.

Between 1885, when the Canadian sealing industry was launched, and 1911, when Canada withdrew from the seal hunt, no fewer than 125 sealing vessels were built in BC, many in makeshift and obscure yards. These ships were alike: strong, sturdy, simple. Sail-powered, they were between 60 and 80 feet long. They were also beamy, which made them good craft in the rough waters of the Bering Sea where the bulk of the seals were taken. Sailors on the best of these craft, it was said, could wear carpet slippers on deck and never get them wet.

One of these ships was the *Beatrice*. By any measure a remarkable vessel, the *Beatrice* laboured at so many tasks that its registry reads like a mongrel's genealogy: sealer, towboat, fish packer, marine research platform. It was also lucky, outlasting several generations of the seamen who trod its plank decks. Like a centenarian peasant who attributes her longevity to a daily stint cutting cordwood, the *Beatrice* survived on work, work, work.

The Canadian sealing industry was a decade old when the *Beatrice* was launched, from James Doherty's False Creek Shipyard in April 1891. The harvest centered around the migratory habits of *Callorhinus ursinus*, or the northern fur seal, whose undercoat of short soft fur was prized by furriers and costumers. Roaming over the North Pacific in search of food, the animals gathered by the hundreds of thousands each summer at the breeding grounds around the Pribilof Islands in the Bering Sea.

BEAMY AND DEEP OF DRAFT, THE *BEATRICE* WAS STABLE IN ALL BUT THE WORST OF WEATHER.

Until the breeding grounds were pinpointed, sealing was a chancy harvest, limited by the sealers' ability to find and keep up with the swift-moving herds. Then in 1885, two vessels, the *Favorite*, from Sooke, and the *Mary Ellen*, from Victoria, returned from the Bering Sea with 4,382 skins, worth an astounding $35,000. The industry exploded; by 1892, 122 schooners with three thousand men were taking part in the pelagic seal hunt. The ships ranged throughout the North Pacific, scouring the waters off the Aleutians and down the Siberian coast to Japan.

The *Beatrice* made a number of runs to the sealing grounds—all were more remarkable for accident or intrigue than for harvest. The first trip was under the registry of Charles G. Doering, a Vancouver brewer and rose gardener par excellence, and his bearded, barrel-chested father-in-law, Hans Helgesen, whose long and varied career matched that of the *Beatrice*. Doering bought the ship to make money; Helgesen was in it, as a son later said, to "have one last fling at the sea."

Helgesen was born in a small town west of Christiania, now Oslo, Norway. His father was a farmer and shipbuilder. He had first gone to sea in 1847, at age eighteen. He joined a sailing ship and worked his way via Cape Horn to the American west coast. In San Francisco he caught word of the California gold rush and jumped ship, walking ashore on a pier made out of cookstoves. He panned for gold in California, then came north on the *Brother Jonathan*. In Victoria he built a scow and made his way to Hope. For several summers he panned gold on the Fraser River, camping and keeping company with a polyglot collection of adventurers. On one of the expeditions a companion of Helgesen's shot a caribou—which is, according to one story, how the Cariboo region got its name.

Gold gave way to farming and an unsuccessful attempt at a sedentary life. In 1862 Helgesen bought a fertile section of ground on a south-facing hill in Metchosin, on southern Vancouver Island. Several years later he left to go prospecting in Nevada, followed by a stint cod fishing in the Queen Charlotte Islands. Cod fishing gave way to provincial politics, which gave way to mining in British Guiana. Between stops at Metchosin to father seven children, he had a mini-career as a fisheries overseer on the Skeena River and revisited a lost gold lode in the Cariboo.

Helgesen was sixty-two when he and Doering purchased the *Beatrice*. He knew local waters and had hoped to captain the vessel. But he lacked proper papers. Reluctantly, he hired a Captain Bjaerre, a Danish deep-sea sailor with papers but no local knowledge. Under Bjaerre's command (and Helgesen's watchful eye) the *Beatrice* departed Victoria and headed south until it intercepted the seal herd off California. Then it turned and followed the herd north.

Seamen have long known that a ship owner and a captain make a volatile combination. Authority is vested in one by proprietorship, in the other by tradition. The two mix like guns and religion. Aboard the *Beatrice*, Helgesen had a number of complaints about the way Bjaerre was handling his ship. He thought it was carrying too much sail, and was sometimes near capsizing. He said as much to Bjaerre, but Bjaerre insisted he knew what he was doing. He didn't.

Two hundred nautical miles off the Queen Charlotte Islands the *Beatrice* hit a severe storm. While the little schooner ploughed into the heavy seas, Bjaerre ordered the fore and aft staysails set. The wheel was lashed to keep the seas just off the bow. Then he and the crew went below to ride out the storm huddled around the tiny wood stove. Helgesen, too, was below deck. His philosopher's brow furled in thought, he watched the flickering oil lamp and listened to the ship's groaning timbers. As usual, he did not like the situation. Only this time he was convinced Bjaerre's boldness—Helgesen would have called it foolishness—was going to end in calamity. The captain had too much sail forward. The risk was that the schooner would pay off—turn broadside to the weather. Once broadside, all it needed was a large wave to send it somersaulting.

The further the *Beatrice* rode into the storm, the more Helgesen fretted. Finally he donned his heavy oilskins and clambered onto the deck. The only other person there, according to Helgesen's account, was the cabin boy, Joe Devine, who was clearing food scraps. The two were clinging to the rails, watching the sails, when Helgesen spotted a wall of water looming on the windward side. It was what seamen call a rogue wave—a freak of wind and current. Helgesen only had time to bellow and take cover. A gust turned the schooner broadside, the wave hit, and everything was sent spiralling. Devine was launched into the sea. Helgesen, clutching a belaying pin, was dragged underwater as the ship capsized. Below decks, the crew were sent tumbling—

down onto the galley ceiling. (The ceiling sported their marks for years.)

How long the *Beatrice* stayed under no one knows—for later all felt it was days. But slowly, freighted by wet sail in water, it righted. As the rigging emerged it scooped the flailing Devine and hoisted him aloft. Stunned, the lad was left straddling a backstay. Like the rest of the crew, he was thankful to be alive. From that point on, Bjaerre and Helgesen appear to have had a more harmonious relationship.

Out on the sealing grounds, the *Beatrice* operated much like any other sealing vessel. At the cry "Boats Out!" the sealers clambered over the side of the ship and into specially designed craft they called shells. It took three men to handle a shell: a steersman or gaffer, a rower and the hunter. Some Native hunters used shells, but most preferred canoes. Canoes carried two, the hunter and a paddler. The paddler was often the wife of the hunter. Once overboard, the canoes and shells fanned from the mother ship. The search for seals often took sealers 15 nautical miles away, until the *Beatrice*'s masts were sticks on the horizon. Each boat was provisioned with a keg of water, hardtack, bully beef and, if the ship's cook was up early enough, prune pie, which was a staple of the sealing fleet. Only the captain and the cabin boy remained on the schooner.

Sealers divided their quarry into three categories: travellers, seals who raced through the water, jumping from wave to wave; moochers, lollygagging seals who raised their heads now and then to look around; and sleepers, who lay on their backs snoozing. Sleepers made up the bulk of seals taken. Hunters had to approach silently, so as not to waken the animal. When the craft was close enough the hunter raised the spear, took aim and sunk the metal tip deep into the seal's blubbery side. It was then the gaffer's job to gaff the seal and haul it to the boat. If the gaffer missed, the seal sank. Some hunters shot bullets into the water to force seals under. After several panicked dives the mammals were too exhausted to evade the spear. When guns were prohibited in the harvest, hunters attached a rope to the weapon's stock. If a patrol boat approached, the gun was lowered over the side.

The first seals caught each day were left whole, for ballast. Any other seals were skinned on sight, the hunter taking care to leave plenty of blubber to insulate the hide from the burning effect of salt, which separated layers of pelts in the hold of the sealing ship. For the first fifty sealskins taken, the hunter received two dollars per head; for the next fifty, three dollars; after a hundred skins the hunter received four dollars apiece.

The money had to be good because the job was hazardous. The North Pacific is not a good place to be in a small boat. Among the many dangers hunters faced, the

THE *BEATRICE* AS A SEALING SCHOONER.

greatest was fog. Great banks of impregnable white mist rolled over the Bering Sea with such frequency the area was known as the Smoky Sea. Within moments a crew with a clear view of the mother ship would be lost. The greatest aid in overcoming the difficulties of navigating in fog was the intuitive sense of the hunters, some of whom accurately guided their tiny boats though thick fog for several hours to arrive at the side of their ship. The mother ships, too, attempted to help crews home. After the small boats pulled away in the morning, the captain would take the ship downwind, so the shells and canoes were likely to blow to it rather than away from it. If visibility was poor at the end of the day the schooner fired guns, and the cabin boy was sent aloft to light an oily rag at the masthead.

Back on the ship, unskinned seals were stripped and their hides salted and stowed. It was a grim site, even by the standards of the day. Author Jack London, who in 1893 travelled for seven months on the sealing schooner *Sophia Sutherland*, described the scene in his book *Sea Wolf*: "It was wanton slaughter... No man ate of the seal meat or the oil. After a good day's killing I have seen our decks covered with hides and bodies, slippery with fat and blood, the scuppers running red; masts, ropes, and rails splattered with the sanguinary color; and the men, like butchers plying their trade, naked and red of arm and hand, hard at work with ripping and flensing knives, removing the skins from the pretty sea creatures they had killed." For London, the horrors of the skinning were compounded by the fact that the entire enterprise was done in the name of fashion, so that the skins "might later adorn the fair shoulders of the women in cities."

On August 20, 1895, the *Beatrice*, under Captain Louis Olsen (and new owners), was working near the Pribilof Islands when it was boarded by American revenue officers from the cutter *Rush*. The *Rush* was one of several American and British gunships in the area, enforcing the terms of the Tribunal of Arbitration at Paris, an 1891 accord that attempted to regulate the harvest. The sealing nations had agreed that all vessels must keep official logs of the harvest and must present the logs for inspection.

In truth, however, the boarding was part of a systematic harassment of sealing ships by American officials. In 1886 the US, afraid of losing a virtual monopoly on sealing, attempted to ban all foreign harvesting, claiming, ludicrously, that since the seals were born on American lands, they were domestic animals. The Russians, who formerly owned Alaska and had tried the same manoeuvre, reminded the Americans

SEALERS ABOARD A VESSEL IN THE SMOKY SEA. THE HARD MASCULINE LIFE APPEALED TO AUTHOR JACK LONDON, BUT EVEN HE FOUND THE SLAUGHTER EXCESSIVE.

of the illegality of their position, and the Americans grudgingly changed their policy—but only technically. In the hold of the *Beatrice* American officers discovered a number of sealskins not entered in the official log. The ship was seized and, following the protocol set up at the Tribunal of Arbitration at Paris, handed over to a British patrol vessel. It was sailed to Victoria where the skins were sold. The Crown then brought charges against the ship's owners. As punishment for not maintaining an accurate log, the Crown asked the courts to order the ship sold. The owners and the captain were outraged. In court, lawyers for the defence testified that the captain had kept perfect records. The mix-up occurred, they said, because it was a temporary log; when the captain had a moment he would have transferred this information into the official log. He had recorded all the information required, but not in the right place.

The judge sitting before the case was unimpressed with the Crown's arguments. He declared the arrest of the *Beatrice* and her detention to be unlawful. Furthermore, the judge said that the *Beatrice* was in pursuit of profit and might reasonably have expected further profit. The Crown was ordered to pay $3,163.50 in damages.

Predictably, the judgment made the *Beatrice* a marked ship on the sealing grounds. The following season, on August 5, 1896, an American patrol boat seized it again, this time for killing seals in a prohibited area. Once more the vessel was transferred to Her Majesty's Service and sailed to Victoria. In court, the captain's defence was that overcast skies made it impossible to properly determine his position. He said that a strong current must have nudged the *Beatrice* into the no-hunting zone. The judge pointed out that it was seized 6 nautical miles within the prohibited area, the logbook contained scratches and crossed-out areas that suggested hasty alteration, and the master's testimony in court was at odds with his own records. The defence collapsed and the owners were required to pay a £400 fine.

By 1911 it was clear that the seal population was seriously depleted. Where it had numbered in the millions in the 1870s, it was

now estimated to be only 150,000. Japan, Canada (represented by Britain), Russia and the United States signed the International Pelagic Sealing Treaty. This treaty ruled that the Bering Sea was to be closed to all pelagic (open ocean) hunting of seals for the next fifteen years. The aboriginal inhabitants of the area were permitted to hunt using traditional methods, i.e. with spear and canoe. Americans could take a limited number of seals on the Pribilof Islands, and the Russians on Robbens Island. In return for keeping its ships from the sealing grounds, Canada was to be given 15 percent of the catch.

Thus, with the signing of the treaty in July 1911, thousands of men lost their

(TOP) IN THE RUSH OF THE HUNT, SLAUGHTERED SEALS WERE OFTEN HEAPED ON THE DECK OF A SEALING SHIP UNTIL THERE WAS TIME TO SKIN AND SALT THE PELTS.

(BOTTOM) AFTER A DAY'S HUNT, SEALERS SKIN THEIR CATCH.

livelihood. Valuable schooners became floating liabilities. Some, like the *Borealis*, were converted into halibut schooners. Others became rumrunners. Many rotted. The *Beatrice* was rescued from the boneyard when the Butchart family set it to work as a lighter in Saanich Inlet. In 1908 it was bought by Captain Albert Berquist of Sidney, on Vancouver Island. Berquist rebuilt boats for a hobby and a living. He was helped by his sister, a fantastically strong woman who could push a shipwright's plane as well as any man. The two cut down the *Beatrice*'s masts, built a deckhouse and installed a 200-horsepower oil-burning steam engine. Thus began the *Beatrice*'s career as a tug. Among its owners were:

Captain John D. Goodwin. Fastidious to the point of insanity, Goodwin was good to his boats but hard on anyone who worked on them. Once Goodwin took some of the *Beatrice*'s machinery to BC Marine Engineers and Shipbuilders for repairs. Goodwin would not let the parts out of his sight, insisting on sitting, hour after hour, on a stool and watching. Understandably, this got on the machinists' nerves. During lunch break one machinist manufactured an especially fine pin, which he fixed to the stool. Goodwin returned, sat down, got up and left.

Sparkie New. A pioneer in BC's towboating industry, Sparkie (Oswald H.) New used the *Beatrice* for towing logs. He once recalled its unusual machinery:

> The *Beatrice* had two hundred pounds working pressure and a compound engine to accept it. Compounds don't ordinarily accept pressures like that, you need a triple expansion job. What they did in this case was to bush the high pressure cylinder down to a much smaller diameter, and then they took the big expansion from that one to the low pressure cylinder. It worked fine, it was very efficient. This was the sort of thing they did in those days, they had lots of imagination.

Harold Clay. Short and litigious, Clay bought the *Beatrice* in 1962. The ship had been gutted by fire while laid up at the North Vancouver ferry dock in 1958. At the time the fire appeared disastrous, destroying the wheelhouse and much of the deck. In the long term, though, the blaze may have done for the old ship what fires do to grassland—reinvigorated it. Clay rebuilt the wheelhouse and refitted the ship with a diesel engine. He changed the name to the *Arrawac Freighter* and chartered it to the Logger's Freight Service, carrying everything from frozen strawberries to diesel engines upcoast. The 900-nautical-mile, sixty-five-stop route was supposed to take five days,

CHILDREN USE THE FORMER SEALER *DIANA* AS A DIVING PLATFORM. MANY SEALING SHIPS WERE LAID UP AFTER 1911 AND LEFT TO ROT.

but Clay's captain had a fondness for carousing logging-camp cooks, which often slowed the journey by a day and a half. On the return to Vancouver, the crew sometimes faced an additional wait if the tide was too low to get the ship over a reef barring the route to its False Creek dock. The rule was: seven planks showing on the rail bridge buttress and the ship cleared the reef; eight planks showing and there wasn't enough water. But rules, explained Clay's captain, don't apply to horny seamen a pike-pole throw from a warm squeeze. He took the *Arrawac Freighter* up to a mighty 8 knots, bounced the keel over the bottom, then idled gracefully to the dock.

Joe Moyles. Keen to use the *Arrawac Freighter*'s ample hold, Moyles bought the ship in 1972 and set it to packing sea urchins and clams on Vancouver Island's west coast. One day smoke billowed from the engine room. The crew bailed into a lifeboat and rowed away, leaving the old ship to gently chug into a fog bank. A few minutes later the *Arrawac Freighter* nosed out of the fog, smokeless, still running. The perplexed crew rowed alongside, caught a line and continued with their work.

By the 1960s the *Beatrice* (for that is what many still called it) was regarded as a coastal veteran, a working maritime museum. Old-time towboaters crossing its wake took their bearings from the ship's past, much as families use their children's progress through grade school to order their memories. In 1971 the *Beatrice*'s reputation as a classic was formalized when the trade newspaper *The Fisherman* declared it one of the oldest working ships on the coast. If the paper's editors were impressed with the ship's longevity, however, they were not awed by its appearance. With warped timbers and rusty, rotting bilge, it looked as if it might sink at dockside. The editors wrote: "The old *Beatrice* deserves a few words before she goes to meet the almost inevitable fate of rotting away in some backwater." They should have known better than to bury a ship older than many churches. The *Beatrice* still had more than two decades of work ahead of it.

In 1981 the *Arrawac Freighter* was bought by Doug Hartley. A slim man with a wheelhouse slouch, Hartley had a marine pedigree that rivalled the *Beatrice*'s. His interest in ships dated to his youth, when he built three boats, including a 24-footer, in his backyard. He went to work on the water, earning a 350-ton Home Trade master's ticket and, later, a degree in marine sciences from the University of Victoria. He has commanded many ships, including the *Sea Lion*, a pioneering tug converted to a research vessel.

Hartley had just obtained plans for a 48-foot schooner from former sealer and renowned boat designer Frank Fredette when the *Arrawac Freighter* came up for sale.

THE *BEATRICE* AS THE *ARRAWAC FREIGHTER*, AT VICTORIA, 1969.

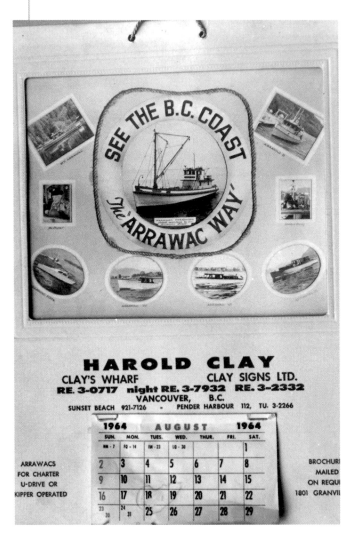

THE *ARRAWAC FREIGHTER*, THE FLAGSHIP OF HAROLD CLAY'S HUMBLE FLEET, IS SHOWN HERE IN THE CENTRE OF A 1964 CALENDER.

He knew the potential hazards of buying an old boat, but the allure was too much. He renamed the boat the *Beatrice* and used it for a number of purposes, including training oceanographers from Royal Roads Military College. Big and stable, it was ideal for the students' green stomachs, especially when they had to work off the West Coast. Once, the *Beatrice* was taking students out from Ucluelet. "There was a big swell and ninety percent of the cadets on the other boats were sick," Hartley recalled. "We came in looking perfectly happy—the other guys couldn't believe it."

The *Beatrice*'s semi-retirement ended in the early 1990s, when Hartley sold it to David Francis of Sardis. A former urchin diver, Francis ran the ship as a packer, working, he says, from Sooke in the south to Zayas Island near Dixon Entrance in the north. It collected urchins from smaller boats and ran the catch to a nearby dock, where they could be trucked to Vancouver for processing. In the days before licensing restrictions, it hauled as much as 75,000 pounds of urchins in a single trip.

The work was rough, but Francis hoped it would be temporary. His goal was to pay the ship off, then charter it out for gentler work. Though not a wooden-boat fanatic, he grew to love the ship. "You've heard of Kodak moments?" he asks. "I've had Kodak weeks out there." When the weather was fine, and the water "flat as piss on a plate," Francis put the *Beatrice* on autopilot and stood on the bow.

Francis skippered the *Beatrice* on every trip—except the last. In April 1993, the *Beatrice* snapped its reverse gearshaft and put into Prince Rupert for repairs. Francis, whose wife was ill, flew home. When the shipyard called early to say the ship was ready, Francis told his engineer to take it across to the Queen Charlottes to fetch a load of urchin. On the way back the ship was caught in a gale. When the engine made an unusual sound the engineer went to investigate. The engine room was thigh deep in water. A hull plank had opened and water was coming in so fast two pumps could not keep up. The engine flooded out. The engineer called mayday. An urchin boat took the foundering ship in tow but was unable to make headway. Another, larger boat hooked on and made for Masset. Meanwhile, the *Beatrice* was slowly sinking. By the time the ship reached the dock the stern was awash. The vessel was secured with heavy lines and the crew left. But it was too heavy. The hawsers snapped and the *Beatrice* rolled into the current, where it was swept away.

In the meantime, Francis, who had been alerted to the crisis, flew to the Queen Charlotte Islands. He hitchhiked to Masset and went to the police. "They told me the boat was gone," he says. "I said, 'What do you mean?' They said it was gone."

Francis went to the dock. Nothing. Using a sounder he scanned Masset Inlet for the hull, but came up empty. The only evidence the *Beatrice* had ever existed was some flotsam from the wheelhouse.

Five years later, Francis and his wife were still living with the legacy of the accident. Because there wasn't a ticketed master on board when the *Beatrice* ran into trouble, there was no insurance. A second mortgage was paying off the ship. Then, too, there was the burden of sinking one of the oldest vessels on the coast. "I still feel real guilt over that," said Francis, who went to work at a youth detention centre in the Fraser Valley. "It was around for a long time."

THE *BEATRICE* AND THE SUBMERSIBLE *DEEP ROVER* WORKING ON THE VANCOUVER ISLAND PIPELINE, NEAR TEXADA ISLAND, C. 1990.

Columbia

G reat journeys in BC are more likely to begin with a vigorous yank on an outboard engine than with the proverbial single step. That's how John Antle, a slender, cocksure minister of the Anglican Church, began his odyssey. Late in the afternoon of June 1, 1904, he scooted a 16-foot cutter named the *Laverock* into the water off a Vancouver beach, leapt into the stern and yarded mightily on the Springfield three-quarter-horsepower outboard. It sputtered to life and Antle set a course of northwest.

"[Y]OU WENT WITH THE TIDE, YOU WAITED FOR THE TIDE, AND SOMETIMES YOU PRAYED FOR THE TIDE." —MARGARET CRAVEN, *I HEARD THE OWL CALL MY NAME.*

JOHN ANTLE AND HIS SON IN
THE *LAVEROCK*, NEAR
CORMORANT ISLAND, 1904.

Antle, or Reverend John, as he was known, was off on a 440-nautical-mile journey (he called it a "spiritual survey") to the logging camps and settlements north of Vancouver. He had heard of the wretched, depraved conditions afflicting Natives and loggers upcoast and thought he would make a reconnaissance himself. For crew he had his nine-year-old son, Victor. For supplies he had a red air cushion, some rough bedding and an Old Testament belief that God would see him out of any fixes.

It was not long before his faith was tested.

Arriving at the Stuart Island end of Cordero Channel north of the Strait of Georgia, Antle was disheartened to see he had missed running the Yuculta Rapids at slack water. The flood was in full force; currents boiled through the river-sized cataract, sending logs, flotsam and eddies swirling in a dizzy tumult. Yet Antle, who had earned his captain's papers on an Atlantic tug, motored in.

He recounted the experience in his journal:

The rapids were running very strong in the flood. How strong we did not know, and its crooked course being over two miles, it was impossible to see...Soon we began to see the whirls and turmoil beyond Dent Island...If there is anyone who thinks he can steer clear of the whirlpools of this rapid in a strong floodtide, he has my permission to try. We skimmed along the edge of several big ones, looking with dread into their funnel-like depths, with the question in our minds: How long before we shall take a header into one? Sure enough, almost immediately we found our little vessel at an angle of 30 or 40 degrees, skimming around the edge of a big one. Finally we crashed to the bottom of it with a bang against a chunk of wood, which shook every timber in the little ship. The boy was yelling at the top of his voice and grabbing his cushion, while I, less articulate but just as scared, wondered how far down we should go. But to our great surprise and relief the smash into the bottom of the pool destroyed its whirling motion and we were suddenly on a flat surface, the engine and sail both still doing business. Verily, there is a Providence who takes care of children and fools, and both were in that boat.

Upcoast, the *Laverock* nosed into backwater bays and timber-fringed inlets in search of settlements. It found many. Though Antle had tended to his ministry in gun-happy US frontier towns and smallpox-wracked Newfoundland outports, nothing could have prepared him for what he now saw. In Native villages, tubercular children withered away under sputum-covered bedsheets. At the Alert Bay Industrial School, he dined alongside a boy whose face and neck were thick with suppurating sores. In logging camps, too, the conditions were beyond imagining. Antle saw firsthand the unheated barns that served as bunkhouses, their hastily constructed walls straining rather than stopping the cold winter winds. At cookhouse dining tables he heard tales of injured men suffering for days after an accident, their open wounds staunched with flour and tourniqueted with a dirty shirt. And then, at a Rock Bay hotel, he observed how the loggers' hard-won money was spent—in a massive run-the-caulk-boots-up-the-wall drunk.

Antle returned to Vancouver on a westerly, convinced there was a role—a need, even—for the church upcoast. But as he explained to a diocese committee studying expansion, it could not be a conventional Anglican, Bible-and-good-manners service. It had to be practical. To put religious services before health care was, in Antle's words, "putting the thick end of the wedge first." People upcoast needed doctors, books, civilization. Spiritual allegiance would follow.

With the decision as good as made (at least in Antle's mind), he brazenly set about planning a ship that would serve the church's needs. Sixty feet long, 14 feet in the beam, 4.5 feet deep, it would sleep three and accommodate twenty-five to thirty for meetings. It would carry a large cabin between small fore and aft decks. Sail would augment a small gasoline engine for power. Bent over his desk, Antle drafted in the minutest details of this ideal craft, including a fold-out altar, complete with altar cloth and cross, that could be shipped away in a cupboard.

The committee rejected Antle's boat, but not his scheme for increasing church presence on the coast. A new ship, they said, was too expensive to build and maintain. As an alternative, one committee member suggested the service could make do with a rowboat. Hauled onto the shore, it would make a sturdy tent. Another member wanted the church to buy his 30-foot cruiser, which happened to be for sale. Someone else suggested using a sealing ship. Antle waved off each suggestion like a

JOHN ANTLE, THE ANGLICAN MINISTER WHO TOOK THE *COLUMBIA* UP AND DOWN THE BC COAST, PROVIDING MEDICAL AND SPIRITUAL SERVICES.

camper swinging at flies. When the committee would not reconsider his original plan, Antle rose from the meeting, grinding his wooden chair angrily on the floor. "Gentlemen, these are my plans," he said, gesturing with a weather-worn hand to the pencilled drafts coiled on the table. "I am not a cheap man and I will not touch a cheap outfit. Good evening." Then he strode from the room. The next day the humbled committee advised Antle that his proposal had been accepted in its entirety.

From Antle's efforts emerged, a year later, the *Columbia*. Strong and seaworthy, the *Columbia* was built at Wallace Shipyards in Vancouver's False Creek. The firm's Old World shipwrights crafted the hull, then constructed a warren of staterooms, an operating "theatre" and a library. When it was launched, a thousand of the city's Anglican upper crust joined shipwrights and boatyard crews at the dock. Antle's wife swung the bottle, which was filled with Lithia water instead of the traditional champagne. It smashed and the boat slid into the water to cheers and hoorays. The next day water was discovered in the new ship's hull. A tradition-minded accomplice of Antle's quipped, "What can you expect but defective waterworks when you give a boat Lithia water at her launching?"

The *Columbia* established regular medical and spiritual services in an area where none existed. Its routes, which stretched between Georgia and Queen Charlotte straits, led the way for a raft of other Columbia Coast Mission boats: the *Columbia II*, the *Makehewi*, the *Fredna*—all known collectively as "God's little ships." The *Columbia* led to the construction of coastal hospitals and the establishment of missions. Though now often derided for its role in subverting Native culture, there is no doubt the CCM was a powerful force in coastal history. The *Columbia* was, to borrow from Antle's practical lexicon, the thin edge of a great wedge.

The vessel's first run was to Victoria. Among the guests who trooped on board in the capital was Captain John T. Walbran, who was compiling the classic book *British Columbia Coast Names*. Walbran, captain of the steam-powered survey ship *Quadra*, had never been on a large gas-powered craft. He was fascinated by the 20-horsepower Union snarling in the stern. It made a lot of noise but not much smoke, the opposite of a steam engine. On the way back to harbour, Captain Walbran joined Antle in the wheelhouse. As the ship neared the dock, Antle rang "Stop" to the engine room and the engineer threw out the clutch, disengaging the propeller but leaving the engine to roar. Walbran was used to the silence of steam. As Doris Andersen recounted in *The Columbia is Coming!*, when the boat neared the dock Walbran could not

THE *COLUMBIA* WAS LAUNCHED FROM WALLACE SHIPYARDS IN FALSE CREEK.

contain himself. "Stop your engines, man!" he bellowed. "You'll ram the dock!" Antle idly spun the wheel. "All in good time, Captain," he answered calmly. Then he rang two bells astern, and brought the ship gently alongside.

The *Columbia*'s gas engine was, in every sense of the phrase, a mixed blessing. Antle wanted it because of the advantages of gas over steam. A steam engine required someone on board to maintain pressure or else took several hours to get steam up. A gas engine could be started on a moment's notice. In the kind of service the *Columbia* was intended for—many starts, many stops—gas seemed ideal.

And it was—as long as the engine behaved. But the Union was stubborn, often refusing to start, like Antle, on matters of principle alone. After several famous outbursts, Reverend John relinquished control of the engine to the *Columbia*'s on-board physician, Dr. W.A.B. Hutton. A quiet man with a disarming gaze, Hutton had arrived on the coast via an alcoholic slide that had destroyed medical careers in Manitoba and Washington state. He was holed up near Halfmoon Bay on the Sunshine Coast, working as a woodcutter, when Antle recruited him. Patient and thoughtful, Hutton joked that he could have Antle defrocked for the language he heard vented in the engine room. He was the only man who mastered the Union's irrational tendencies.

On its regular run, the *Columbia* serviced about fifty-six ports of call between Pender Harbour in the south and Port Hardy, at the northern tip of Vancouver Island. It stopped at Ben Willet's Camp, George O'Brien's Camp, Scott's Camp, and lighthouses at Pine Island and Scarlett Point. It stopped at Native communities too: Village Island, Karlukwees, Kingcome, Fort Rupert and Nahwitti.

At each port of call the two-man crew split up and tended to their respective duties. Skipper-cum-priest held a service or, in the poker- and whiskey-minded logging camps, tried at least to strike up conversations that touched on such subjects as ethics, responsibility and morals. Meanwhile, engineer-cum-doctor Hutton was yanking abscessed teeth, lancing boils and checking newborns. How long the ship remained at dock depended on the tenacity of the molar roots, the interest of the locals in Antle's discourses. The ship had a route and a schedule, but these were abandoned whenever an emergency arose. During one eight-day stretch, the ship carried eight injured loggers from camps to the hospital at Rock Bay. The timetable

(TOP) THE *COLUMBIA* EMBODIED THE COLUMBIA COAST MISSION'S UNOFFICIAL MOTTO: SERVICE, NOT SERVICES.

(BOTTOM) PHYSICIAN, WOODCUTTER, MECHANIC— W.A.B. HUTTON'S ABILITY WITH THE *COLUMBIA*'S GAS ENGINE MEANT JOHN ANTLE COULD CONCENTRATE ON HIS MINISTRY.

was obliterated but Antle could not have been more pleased. He always said the *Columbia*'s first task was to provide service, not services.

Working in the *Columbia*'s tight quarters, Dr. Hutton and, later, Dr. D.P. Hanington tended to every sort of ailment. According to the CCM newsletter, *The Log*, in October 1906 the patients included Jack Whipple, Camp D, "struck by chain hook, lost most of foot"; William Lewis, of Paterson's camp, "injured thumb, 14 stitches"; C. Berlingson, "fell with a tree, internal injuries and broken wrist"; I. Teepan of Cracroft Island, "broken collarbone"; Pat Diffley, "broken rib, torn lung"; and John Norberg of Thurlow Island Logging camp, "severe axe wound."

The *Columbia* was docked at Norton and McKinnon's Sunderland Camp when Hanington was called on to tend a uniquely coastal injury. While Antle and the doctor chatted with the camp supervisor, George Fraser, after dinner, William Norton and Jack Bennet scaled a hill to blast a stump with dynamite. There was an explosion, then nothing. After an hour several men investigated. Bennet had been torn apart in the blast, but Norton was alive, mangled and nearly frozen. With only the *Columbia*'s rudimentary supplies to work with, Hanington kept Norton alive until he could be transferred to a hospital. Several months afterward a note in *The Log* registered the crew's thanks. "I am instructed [by the crew]," wrote George Fraser, "to put down in good plain English the most emphatic approval of Dr. Hanington's splendid work in the two days and nights he was at the bedside, and am to 'see that they print it in *The Log*'."

Hutton not infrequently acted as confessor to Antle who, for all his blowing, was deeply insecure. From the very first trip in the *Columbia*, Antle admitted to Hutton, he had wondered if the medicine-first, God-later approach was wise. Was the CCM right to use church money—bequeathed by good Anglicans in Edenbridge—to run the *Columbia*'s blasphemy-inspiring gas engine? How far could service be stretched in God's name? Hutton responded in a breezy, good-tempered manner. "Heal the sick," Andersen quotes him recalling from St. Luke, "and say unto them, the kingdom of God is come nigh unto you. Heal their bodies and the rest will follow."

It didn't hurt Antle's conscience that the *Columbia* was able to engage in traditional religious work, too. Between turns as an ambulance, it served as a floating church. If the *Columbia* was docked at a small settlement, the whole population might be invited aboard. Two or three families, smelling of wood smoke and work, crowded into the cabin. Antle performed the service, then there were prayers and singing.

COLUMBIA COAST MISSION SKIPPERS WERE ADVISED TO "READ YOUR TIDE BOOK AS OFTEN AS YOUR BIBLE."

At larger settlements—meaning more than twenty people—the service was held ashore. Some of the most memorable services were conducted on beaches. The *Columbia*'s portable organ, known as "Little Jimmy," was trundled along a slippery boomstick and set up amid the sand and clamshells. The combination of song and scene, underlaid by musical foundation from "Little Jimmy," was a magical respite from the slog of homesteading in the rainforest.

The *Columbia*'s sermon-on-a-stump style of religion appealed to loggers, as well. After Antle retired, CCM reverends liked to tell a story about an "unnamed" priest aboard the *Columbia* who was conducting his sermon on the beach. He had just commenced when a call for help came through. A man was bust up in the bush miles away. Off went the cassock and surplus, on went the skipper's cap. In minutes the *Columbia* was on its way. Among those observing the rapid transformation was a boozy, cathouse-prone logger who had been dragged to the service. "That," he growled, watching the ship disappear around a distant bluff, "is the best damned sermon I ever heard."

Antle may have been "through the ringbolts," as Newfoundland sailors said of an experienced mariner, but the Pacific coast was still a treacherous place to run a boat early in this century. Hydrographic surveys were incomplete or, worse still, flawed. Passages shown as clear on charts too often sheltered underwater promontories, reefs, wrecks—the kinds of obstructions that tore the bottom from a boat or plucked propellers from their shafts. The lore that mariners pass to one another about eddies and rips and shoals was still unfolding. The British Admiralty's hydrographic office cancelled some charts with a warning that they were "so inaccurate as to be positively dangerous to use for any navigation."

Between the hazards of an imperfectly charted coast and a temperamental engine, it was inevitable the *Columbia* would run into trouble. In February 1909, the

THE BIBLE BARGE *COLUMBIA* AT A TYPICAL COASTAL DOCK.

BIGGER AND BETTER
EQUIPPED, THE *COLUMBIA II*
WORKED FOR THE COLUMBIA
COAST MISSION UNTIL 1957.

ship was on an emergency run to Cape Scott when the Union engine clattered to a stop. Inspection revealed stripped gears. In a heavy sea the auxiliary sails were set and the ship made for the coast. The ship anchored in a bay, then Antle and the crew rowed to shore and hiked through the salal to the patient's home. In a nearby sawmill they also found tools to fix the *Columbia*. On the row back they hit rough seas. Heavy fog blanketed the shore. A local in the boat, who had been leading the way, confessed to being lost. Antle took charge. He ordered the boat rowed out to sea, then along the coast. When he thought they were off the spot where the *Columbia* was anchored, they turned landward. Slate grey seas slapped at the little boat's sides. "If we hit bottom," Antle muttered, "every man for himself...swim towards the land and God help you."

From the bow came a wail. It was the cook. "I haven't said my prayers for years," he burbled. "This seems to be the time to start again."

Antle looked the man in the eye. "It's hardly playing square with the Lord to wait until you're in a mess like this," he lectured. "Your present job is to keep water out of the boat, so bail!" A navigational combination of prayer and reckoning led them alongside the *Columbia*. The gears were replaced and the mission ship trundled off.

The *Columbia* was not two years old when Antle began planning a boat to replace it. The mission had become so popular that the little vessel could not accommodate the faithful at onboard sermons, and there was not enough room to tend the injured properly. After a vigorous bout of fund-raising, Antle won his new boat. The *Columbia II*, launched in 1910, served the coast well for over fifty years.

In 1910 the original *Columbia* was sold, converted to a pleasure craft, and reregistered as the *Chaos*—a name many thought supremely fitting. In 1914 it was purchased by Harry Morgan of Victoria; in 1925 it was owned by Frank Cvitanovich and Jack Fiomengo of Vancouver. Sometime later it was dismantled. Only the ship's wheelhouse bell survived, enjoying a second career as a dinner gong outside a home at Bliss Landing, a community north of Powell River.

John Antle died in 1949. Four years later the Columbia Coast Mission rebuilt a twelve-year-old vessel and arranged to place the *Columbia*'s bell in it. The vessel was one of several that honoured the name of the mission's driving character. Antle's son was present for the dedication. The ship, which would carry on in the CCM's memorable tradition, was named the *John Antle IV*.

Princess Maquinna

The Canadian Pacific Railway steamer *Princess Maquinna* was called a lot of names in its day: Old Faithful, the Ugly Duckling, the Ugly Princess and, by a one-eyed Irish handlogger, Slatternly Streel. No one ever said it was pretty. The great blackened sides resembled flabby flanks, and the single skinny funnel looked like a ridiculously undersized stovepipe hat. Even the bow, normally the most rakish part of a vessel, was unappealingly perpendicular, as though the ship knew of the uncharted reefs that littered its routes along the west coast of Vancouver Island and was wincing in preparation for a collision.

JAMES TROUP'S CONTRIBUTION TO THE *PRINCESS MAQUINNA*'S DESIGN WAS EVIDENT IN THE LOW SUPERSTRUCTURE AND THE EASY-ACCESS SIDE CARGO DOORS.

Inside was no better. The ship had a single saloon, which doubled as lobby, entrance, newsstand and ticket office. It was decorated with what one traveller generously called an "unlovely" green leather. The leather smelled of loggers. The seats were built around the walls. If the ship was in a heavy sea and one passenger lost his balance, everyone went down like windfall. Adjacent to the lounge was a smoking room, and near that the dining room. Depending on one's notions of comfort, they were snug and homey or small and awful. Near the stern were the cabins, which could only be reached via a labyrinth of zigzag passages, designed, it seemed, to mirror the ship's strange route. The unique arrangements, explained one captain, made for a unique voyage. "There wasn't anywhere else to go," he said. "Everyone had to be friendly."

Despite the *Maquinna*'s eccentricities (or maybe because of them), residents of Vancouver Island's western shores loved the ship the same way they loved the coast. It was a fine affection too, born not from the arrogance of ownership, like the yachtsman's pride, but from more enduring qualities: reliability, longevity, strength, character. From 1913 to 1952, the sturdy ship steamed northwest from Victoria to the towns and camps along the Island's Pacific coast; each year the bond grew stronger. Passengers grew fond of the ship's odd profile and cramped quarters. They even enjoyed the *Maquinna*'s whistle, which misfired on the higher notes, ending in a

screeching falsetto, like a youth whose voice is breaking. It was a whistle only a west-coaster could love.

In maritime genealogy, the *Princess Maquinna* was the linear descendant of the *William Irving* and other sternwheelers from Captain John Irving's Pioneer Line that worked the Fraser River. In 1883 when the Pioneer Line and the Hudson's Bay Company amalgamated to form the Canadian Pacific Navigation Company, what had primarily been a New Westminster–Victoria service was extended to include coastal routes. It was this emerging empire that was purchased, in 1901, by the CPR.

The dominant ideology at the CPR was still expansion. As if building railroads wasn't task enough, the company was spreading into shipping. Between the summer of 1910 and the fall of 1914 the CPR built or purchased eight ships for its local coastal routes. Plotting this expansion was Captain James W. Troup, an American whose father and grandfather were steamboat captains on the Columbia River. A slim figure with an elfin face, Troup started his maritime career as a boy, standing tiptoe on a soapbox and guiding his father's sternwheeler along the river. At twenty-one, he commanded the *Harvest Queen*, one of the largest steamers built in the Northwest. When a railroad rendered upper Columbia River steamboats obsolete, he herded the *Harvest Queen* and other steamers through the white-water cataracts of Celilo Falls and Tumwater Rapids, events with such suicidal promise that several thousand observers were attracted.

The CPR hired Troup primarily for his practical expertise, but he had a talent for naval architecture, as well. He insisted on seeing hull designs and had a deep understanding of what worked and, more importantly, what didn't. During the design of an early CPR boat he happened into the architect's office. Troup picked up the wooden model of the proposed hull, turned it end-over-end, then declared something was amiss. The engineers scurried for their slide rules. Troup was right. The hull had to be redesigned.

Troup insisted the CPR's ships were built—or in the case of purchased vessels, rebuilt—to the finest standards. These craft were a combination of ocean-going liner, coastal steamer and riverboat. From the sternwheeler era he took the idea of a single freight deck. The new ships had a large main deck, accessed by large freight doors, thus avoiding the slow transfer of cargo via winches and derricks. Troup also insisted the ships' sides be perpendicular from the main deck up. This enabled a vessel to come alongside a wharf in heavy seas or high winds—conditions that would have damaged a ship with the more traditional flared hull.

Troup often added other touches to individual ships. His contributions to the *Maquinna*'s design were several: he insisted on a low upper-deck structure to keep the ship from rolling in West Coast swells; he added a sleek stern, which checked the tendency of the stern to rise in heavy seas and allow the propeller to race; he eliminated promenades and large observation windows; and he placed the public rooms amidships, the most comfortable spot in a pitching vessel. The resulting craft, built from imported British steel at BC Marine Railway in Esquimalt, was launched on Christmas Eve 1912. It was christened by Mrs. Fitzerbert Bullen, granddaughter of Sir James Douglas. At the time, it was the biggest ship built in the province.

The *Maquinna* was a calendar to west coasters. Leaving Victoria on the first, eleventh and twenty-first days of each month, it would steam up the coast, stopping at some twenty-five settlements and camps. Even before the ship departed Victoria, you could sense there was something different in the journey ahead. While bureaucrats and the well-heeled filed aboard graceful CPR sister ships bound for other coastal destinations, the *Maquinna*'s decks were a calamity. Guns, boom chains, saws, books and people crammed its decks and holds. It was moored "dockside proper," meaning it was tied alongside the dock and was loaded and unloaded via a gangplank.

BACKED BY THE CPR'S DEEP POCKETS, CAPTAIN TROUP BUILT THE CANADIAN PACIFIC NAVIGATION COMPANY'S SMALL FLEET INTO THE DOMINANT PASSENGER/CARGO SERVICE ON THE COAST.

There was none of the security consciousness that has transformed latter-day ship departures into glorified cattle drives. Unticketed guests were invited to mingle on board until minutes before the ship departed. The arrangement suited loggers heading north for six months of work and celibacy. Among the throngs of visitors who left just before the ship departed were many well-dressed but slightly tousled women.

As the only regular passenger vessel running the outer coast, the *Princess Maquinna* was a favourite with tourists. Troup himself had encouraged the company to promote the scenic aspect of the trip. After returning from the ship's first voyage, he wrote to H.W. Brodie, a company passenger agent, that the trip was in many ways better than the CPR's run to Alaska. The company soon began cranking out brochures about the rugged Pacific coast scenery. The names of the stops suggested a journey back in time. From Victoria, the ship's sailing list included: Port Renfrew, Carmanah, Clo-oose, Nitinat, Bamfield, Sarita Bay, Ecoole, Kildonan, Green Cove, Franklin River, Port Alberni, Ucluelet, Tofino, Clayoquot, Kakawis, Ahousat, Hot Springs Cove, Hesquiat, Nootka, Tahsis, Ceepeecee, Esperanza, Hecate, Zeballos and Chamiss Bay.

One thing the publicists never did hype was the waves. Sometimes the *Maquinna* would plough through open seas for hours. After years of swabbing tourist vomit, the crew inveigled the CPR into including the following proviso in its effusive brochures:

> The only drawback is the fact that the steamer is quite often, and sometimes for several hours at a time, in the open Pacific, and even

CROWDS OF NATIVE CANNERY WORKERS ON THE *PRINCESS MAQUINNA* SIGNALLED THE START OF THE FISHING SEASON.

in pleasant weather the ground swell that is always present results in attacks of seasickness with those who are poor sailors. The majority of passengers, however, are not affected, and most of the small minority look upon it as an experience to be talked about on their return home.

For those not bothered by the teeter-totter action of the decks, the trip bested the CPR's promotional promises. After rounding the winking lighthouse at Race Rocks, the ship travelled north and west, often running so close to shore passengers could see spume-wracked rocks and tangles of bone-white driftwood. At Jordan River the low coastal hills of southern Vancouver Island gave way to vertiginous mountains, and the real West Coast began. To many passengers, the journey from Jordan River on was a disquisition on green: iridescent-, glaucous-, sea- and aquamarine-green mountains flowed into an ocean the colour of olive, pea and sage. Greens folded into one another, blurred, melded, shifted with the light. Hallucinatory greens, greens never seen before. Passengers stumbled from the *Maquinna*'s outer decks overwhelmed with green, yarded on the doors, lurched inside... and faced the Christly green chairs. It was a green trip to a green land.

Tourists riding the *Maquinna* for their first time were often surprised to find the crew willing to chat or name passing landmarks. If the weather was pleasant, officers started deck games. When off watch, they dined with the passengers. The captain sat at the head of his table, and the ship's officers, chief engineer and purser sat at other tables in the saloon. Everyone was part of the trip.

Travellers also liked the fact that the *Princess Maquinna* was a working boat. As it steamed upcoast it stopped to unload cargo and passengers. The first call was Port Renfrew, five hours out of Victoria. Port San Juan, as the spot is called locally, is a port in name only; the bay opens directly onto the Pacific swells. The surge made normal docking hazardous. Where three lines would suffice to hold the *Maquinna* at most docks, six were used at Renfrew. Even so, detonating hawsers often sent all hands ducking. Over the years the *Maquinna* lost more lines at Port Renfrew than at all other ports together.

THE *MAQUINNA* SLOGGING THROUGH FOUL WEATHER EN ROUTE TO ANOTHER COASTAL PORT.

The tricks of docking at Port Renfrew were rivalled by the tricks of loading and unloading cargo. Despite Troup's best plans, the cargo doors were useless if a swell was running; unloading was done with a winch. For years the master of the cranes was a silent, stone-faced bachelor named Charles Bertram Wright, known to crewmen as Shorty. Wright was a thick-set man, with immense hands calloused the texture of salmon jerky from cradling his inextinguishable pipe. He had come to Victoria as an orphan from Jersey in the Channel Islands. After decking on several tugs, he had worked on the steamer *Iroquois*, then moved onto CPR boats and the *Maquinna*.

Some people are gifted musicians; others are good with plants. Wright's forte was winches. If the *Maquinna* was heaving at dockside, he would swing a load of groceries over the dock and wait for the ship to go down in a trough. A touch of the controls, a muttered profanity, and the pallet kissed the wharf. When he was on, which was almost always, Wright could move Royal Doulton china without chipping a handle. When he was off, which was rarely, there was catastrophe—cans of milk and other goods splattered all over. Success or failure, his expression never changed. All he ever offered by way of an explanation was a puff on his meerschaum pipe and a thickly accented comment: "It's hit and miss."

Villages such as Clo-oose, with no dock, were called boat landings. The *Maquinna* hove to offshore and canoes paddled out, bows plunging through the swell. In the ship's lee they came alongside the cargo doors. A crewman, harnessed to the hull, leaned out with bundles of goods. Here, the trick was to pass the bundles while the canoe was at the top of a wave. The drama was intensified when a passenger made the transfer from ship to canoe, or canoe to ship. If the canoe was in a trough, the passenger faced a drop of 10 or 12 feet (3 or 4 m); if he or she jumped too soon, the unfortunate soul met the canoe rising on a swell. If the passenger was too old, then Wright deftly lowered a coal bucket over the side, and the decrepit individual climbed in.

Keeping track of the array of cargo in the *Maquinna*'s belly was the purser's job. With so many stops on the route, the purser barely had time to prepare a shipment before the ship lurched against another dock. In the rush, orders got confused. The ship was held up at one stop while the purser and crew rooted around for a crate of shoats. They didn't know what shoats were, so they searched everywhere, including over and under a crate of pigs. It took an officer with a dictionary to solve the mystery. Similarly, the crew hunted in vain for what was described on the manifest as a "crate of ranges." The ranges they knew of were used for cooking. They later discovered the letter "O" had been left off a box of fruit.

The freight deck was a particularly awful place to be in a storm. Crews never did figure out how to make the cargo secure, just as the stewards above never managed to firmly anchor the piano that lived in a corner of the saloon. When the *Maquinna* hit a gale both cargo and piano became animated, much to the consternation of the crew and passengers. In a really heavy storm, the captain would blow the whistle before a particularly large wave struck and everyone took shelter.

The regular next stop after Clo-oose was Bamfield, at the entrance to Barkley Sound. Passengers stretched their legs and chatted with Australian and New Zealand crews who manned the cable station, then the ship carried on to Estevan Point and points north. On the third day of the voyage it steamed from Nootka Cannery to Gordon Gibson's lumber mill at Tahsis and on to Zeballos in Esperanza Inlet. After leaving Zeballos it swung south and followed the same route back.

Between foul weather and unscheduled stops, the *Maquinna* inevitably drifted off schedule. And the farther up the coast it went, the farther it strayed. Residents in remote communities got some inkling of the *Maquinna*'s arrival from the 8 p.m. "Vancouver Province" newscasts on a prominent local radio station. Before recounting the day's news, the program's debonair host, Earle Kelly (also known as "Mr. Good Evening"), would announce the ship's progress: "...at 4 p.m. the good ship *Princess Maquinna* was at Tofino, northbound." The newscasts had the tangential benefit of associating the *Maquinna* with one of BC's most eligible bachelors, as Kelly, a top tennis player, was often seen at nightclubs arm-in-arm with attractive women.

For residents of remote communities, the sound of the *Maquinna*'s whistle brought the promise of shopping, goods, spare parts, new employees, gossip. It was a trip to town, a theatre. Even before the ship was docked, the yacking between passengers, crew and docksiders began: who was dating whom, when which fish boat was due back in port. Then the gangplank was run out and the goods unloaded. Flimsy packing crates were ripped open on the spot and new parts extracted. Inevitably, there was hollering ("Jesus H. Christ, they sent the wrong part!"). There were joyous shrieks from women seeing grandchildren for the first time. Kids surged aboard to buy candy from Joan Leslie, the genial Shetland Islander who ran the ship's concession; their parents ambled in to look at magazines or drifted over to talk with an officer. Sometimes the captain could be persuaded to hold the ship over for a dance. He and his officers and the ship's guests would hike to the local hall to dance and, as all west coasters did, swing until morning. Then residents retired to their beds and the passengers and crew to the ship. It was a uniquely coastal treat to drift off to sleep footsore, hoarse, drunk and listening to the fading echos of the *Maquinna*'s whistle.

Though the *Maquinna* had many captains, old-timers on the coast associated the ship with one man. That was Captain Edward Gillam. Gillam was master of the *Maquinna* from 1913 to 1928. Born in Port aux Basques, Newfoundland, he moved to the West Coast at age sixteen. After a career in the sealing fleet, he joined the Canadian Pacific Navigation Company as a deckhand. In six years he had his master's papers and was given command of the *Queen City*.

An affable man with a habit of rocking on his heels, Gillam was burdened with two tragedies in his life. Both involved water. The first was the drowning, in 1914, of his only son. The second was the wreck of a Chilean sailing ship that ran aground off Tofino.

On November 25, 1919, a heavy storm was setting in over the West Coast when the *Maquinna* cast off from Tofino. Though Gillam had his doubts about the weather, he knew enough about Pacific storms to realize that they can go as fast as they come. Besides, he had not earned a reputation as one of the CPR's most reliable captains by keeping his vessel lashed to the dock. But the farther the *Maquinna* ploughed out of the harbour the more violently the seas broke against the hull. Gillam was just about to order the ship back to Tofino when a large three-masted vessel was spotted lying close to the shore. It was the *Carelmapu*, out of Chile, bound for Puget Sound. It had lost its sails in a storm off Cape Flattery and, without a tug in sight, drifted shoreward. The ship dropped anchors in hopes of holding off the rocks, then as it scudded onto the reefs, hoisted flags upside down, the international code for distress.

In the *Maquinna*'s wheelhouse, Gillam quickly tallied his options. His first responsibility was to his own ship, its passengers and crew. But he had a responsibility to the seamen on board the *Carelmapu*, as well. Without the *Maquinna*'s assistance, their only hope was to get off the ship before it disintegrated in the surf. And the odds of that, Gillam knew, were less than slight. The question was, where did heroism end and recklessness begin? Gillam pondered for a moment, then in his clipped, steady-as-she-goes voice, told his helmsman to make for the foundering ship.

On Gillam's orders, the mate, C.P. Kinney, barked instructions to the crew. All seamen on deck. Every moveable object lashed down. Lifeboats at the ready. Meanwhile, the *Maquinna* slid in among the toothy reefs that thrust out from the shore. Visible one moment, they disappeared under a heavy swell, then surfaced again, shedding white froth. When his ship was 150 yards (165 m) from the *Carelmapu*, Gillam ordered two anchors dropped. The anchor lines came tight with a jerk. That was as far as he dared go.

Over the *Maquinna*'s heaving stern, the crew watched the *Carelmapu* grinding on a reef. Beside the hull they could see an upturned lifeboat, with hats and oars floating nearby. The sea had already claimed five lives. Crews of both ships hollered, but the noise of the breakers, swept by the rising storm, was too thunderous to communicate. Captain Gillam ordered a line and a buoy drifted downwind, but this too failed. A crew volunteered to lower one of the *Maquinna*'s life rafts but, after agonizing for several moments, Gillam refused. Then a big sea hit the *Maquinna* and the wrist-thick anchor lines went taut. The bow heaved and there was a shriek of metal. It was the winches. Strained beyond capacity, they had ripped from the

CAPT. EDWARD GILLAM, MASTER OF THE *MAQUINNA* FROM 1913 TO 1928. IN SIX YEARS WITH THE CANADIAN PACIFIC NAVIGATION COMPANY, HE WORKED HIS WAY UP FROM DECKHAND TO MASTER.

decks like carrots from soft ground then slammed into the hawsepipes. Gillam was now in a perilous position—anchored amid the reefs by gear that could not be raised. Working frantically, Kinney took a hacksaw to the lines. Gillam tried to hold the bow into the swell, marking the shore for a sign they were drifting. After an hour and a half, the anchor lines parted and disappeared into the sea. Relieved, disappointed, exhausted, Gillam gave the order and the *Maquinna* pulled away from the reefs.

Aboard the *Carelmapu* some of the crew, clearly desperate, lowered another life raft. They got away from the big ship but were capsized before reaching shore. All seven died. Another large wave hit the wreck and carried it over a reef. A few hours later, it broke in two. The forepart sank, but the stern lodged among the rocks. As the tide receded, five survivors, including a nineteen-year-old Chilean student on his way to university in Seattle, and a dog made their way ashore. The *Maquinna* never again steamed past the site without Gillam walking to a window and, rocking on his heels, studying the shore for a few moments.

THE DEATH OF A SHIP, AS SEEN FROM THE DECK OF THE *PRINCESS MAQUINNA*. FROM TOP: THE DISABLED SQUARE-RIGGER *CARELMAPU* LOWERS A LIFEBOAT NEAR THE STERN; BOTH ANCHOR LINES SNAPPED, THE SHIP DRIFTS TOWARDS THE ROCKS; THE LIFEBOAT, VISIBLE OFF THE STERN OF THE *CARELMAPU*, MAKES ITS WAY THROUGH THE SURF BEFORE CAPSIZING.

The CPR liked to boast of the regal passengers the *Princess Maquinna* had carried, such as the Marquis of Willingdon and his wife. The marquis, then Governor General of Canada, was taken on a spit-and-polish trip around Vancouver Island. But crews aboard the *Maquinna* had another list. Among their celebrated passengers was a horse. The horse was snuck aboard one night while the ship was in Victoria. The culprits led the nag, head first, into a cabin, then departed and shut the door. When an unusual stink led a crewman to the cabin, there was turmoil. Any thought of reversing the horse out of the cabin was abandoned after a few bone-shattering lashes with its hooves. In the end, the cabin wall was cut away and the horse led out.

Though crews applied paint by the bucketful, by the 1940s nothing could mask the *Maquinna*'s aging. It heaved and groaned, rattled and shook. Even the meals, once a hallmark of *Maquinna*'s service, resembled something served up at a gyppo logging show. The tables were dotted with little water tumblers. The tumblers, rims lined with butter, were designed to catch the cockroaches threatening to take over the ship. Diners had the delight of watching the bugs, tempted by the butter, ascend the glass then plunge in. Once in they could not get out and after much twitching, drowned.

THE *MAQUINNA* ALONGSIDE GILLNETS LAID OUT FOR REPAIR.

Smart-aleck stewards said the bugs were another CPR perk, just like the gut-busting waves.

The aging ship's physical structure was showing wear, too. Plumbing leaked, furniture was dingy. In its final days the *Maquinna* even lost its famed whistle. It was entering a port upcoast. The captain ordered the "entering port" signal. On the bridge the boatswain yanked the cord and the beloved whistle resounded and echoed off the mountains, climbing higher and higher...then it stopped. There was silence. The boatswain pulled again. Nothing. A deckhand was sent to investigate. He discovered the whistle was gone—vanished, as far as anyone could tell, down the smokestack. The *Maquinna* had swallowed its whistle.

The coast was changing, too, and not in ways that favoured steamers. By 1950 floatplanes had replaced the old ships as the favoured mode of transportation. A logging camp could send for crew or parts and have them the same day. The advent of the outboard made it possible for residents to zoom from camp to town and back quickly, as well.

In September 1952, the *Maquinna* was loaded and waiting to depart from Victoria when the captain called the passengers together. The ship's boilers, he said, were unable to get up steam. The ship would stay at dock. The passengers were welcome to spend the night, and they would be fed breakfast, but they had to find another way upcoast.

DECADES OF HEAVY SEAS AND HARD DOCKINGS TOOK THEIR TOLL ON THE *MAQUINNA*'S HULL AND EQUIPMENT. EVEN THE SHIP'S WHISTLE FAILED IN OLD AGE.

In 1953 the *Maquinna* was purchased by the Waterhouse Division of the Union Steamship Company. It was stripped and the engines torn out. Renamed the barge *Taku*, it joined *Bulk Carrier No. 1* (formerly the *Southholm*) and *Bulk Carrier No. 3* (formerly the *Princess Mary*) transporting ore from the Consolidated Mining and Smelting Company's operation at Tulsequah, on the Portland Canal, and Britannia Beach, in Howe Sound, to its smelter in Tacoma. Later, the *Taku* was tied to a buoy in Vancouver harbour until, in 1962, it was towed to False Creek and broken up. Before the cutting torches were loosed on it, there was a brief ceremony to remove the bell. Among those on hand was John Stevenson, who had installed the bell on the *Princess Maquinna* forty-nine years before. The organizers would have liked the venerable Charles Wright to adorn the function, but Shorty was working the winches on another CPR ship.

"OLD FAITHFUL" AS THE BARGE *TAKU*, ALONGSIDE THE FORMER US ARMY TRANSPORT *VETA C.*

Malahat

arrie Nation. Gordon Gibson. Two people could not differ more and still be classified as Homo sapiens. Nation marched the US into Prohibition. Gibson swilled a bottle of scotch a day. Nation attacked city saloons with the cry, "Smash, for the love of the Lord, smash!" Gibson logged the west coast of Vancouver Island and called himself "Bull of the Woods." Nation was small and nasal. Gibson was big and bass-voiced. Nation was prim, Gibson unbuttoned. Yet through the strange architecture of history, both figured in the odd, accidental life of a wooden-hulled schooner, the *Malahat*.

Built in Victoria to carry lumber in World War I, the *Malahat* was saved from oblivion twice: first by American Prohibition, which created a need for ships to lug bootleg liquor to California, and second by Gordon Gibson, the sledgehammer visionary who transformed the ship into the world's first self-propelled, self-loading log carrier in 1936.

THE *MALAHAT* AS IT LOOKED SOON AFTER
LAUNCHING IN 1917.

The *Malahat* was a "Mabel Brown" motor sailer—a crisis-inspired breed of ship hurriedly constructed to replace freighters seconded for the war effort. Fuel-efficient and built of non-strategic lumber, these vessels were nearly identical: 246 feet long, with capacity for up to 1,800,000 board feet of lumber or a large tonnage of general cargo. Their strength lay in their versatility. They were designed to operate under power or sail. In sailor's parlance, the *Malahat* was a five-masted schooner, rigged bald-headed, meaning it carried no topsails. To reduce the need for experienced seamen, the mainsails were hoisted from the deck with steam winches. Though large, the ship had a reputation as a "sweet sailer." When the wind failed, it could run on two cranky Swedish semi-diesel engines that were coaxed to combustion by blow torches welded to each cylinder head.

Launched in 1917, the *Malahat* was dispatched to Australia with a shipment of coastal lumber. Another wartime journey saw it bound for England with a cargo of nitrates. Off the South American coast the crew noticed water leaking into the bilge. Investigation revealed the tropical heat was causing the caulking to come loose. All hands were ordered below to reseal, including M.B. McLaren, an eighteen-year-old sailor from Vancouver. McLaren had gone to sea expecting to scramble around the rigging or, when the wind was fair, repose on deck, plucking his ukelele. Instead, he was dehydrating in a stifling, airless hold. "I can remember caulking in temperatures between 100 and 125 degrees," he recalled years later. "We lads would go almost blind with that tar and sun, and when we couldn't stand it any more we'd go to the

THE MABEL BROWN CLASS
OF MOTOR SAILERS WERE
BUILT ENTIRELY OF WOOD.

fo'csle and stick damp bandages over our eyes until we felt well enough to start all over again." The only time sailors were permitted above deck was to trim the sails or drench themselves in a rare rainstorm. They caught rainwater in canvas sheets and directed the rivulets into buckets for washing and drinking. "It wasn't too bad," McLaren remembered, "except for the brine."

It was on the same 1917 voyage that the *Malahat* had its first and only direct encounter with the war. At Iquique there were twenty vessels already in the harbour: two Allied, eighteen German. Though Chile had interred the German ships, a lack of Chilean soldiers meant German sailors did as they pleased. They roamed the town brandishing sidearms and taunting foreign crews, even before the two Allied vessels steamed out of port. As McLaren discovered, the *Malahat* made an irresistible target.

The *Malahat* was riding at anchor in the crowded harbour. The captain had ordered the crew to keep an extra-sharp watch, in part because of his concerns about sabotage, in part because he was worried about the heavy groundswell. If the ship dragged its anchors, he told the crew, there would be precious little time to respond. It would founder on the rocks or collide with another vessel. Prowling the decks on night watch, McLaren heard the sound of oars dipping nearby. He tiptoed to the

SHIPS' KNEES, L-SHAPED SECTIONS OF WOOD HEWN FROM THE INTERSECTION OF TREE ROOTS AND TRUNK, WERE CRITICAL TO THE *MALAHAT*'S STRENGTH.

gunwales and peered overboard. In the black he made out two rowboats stealthily moving towards the *Malahat*'s anchor cables. He didn't wait to see the uniforms. He bawled an alert that set dogs ashore howling. In moments, the sides of the ship bristled with armed sailors. The rowboats altered course and vanished amid the German ships. To the great relief of all on the *Malahat*, the next day the HMS *Lancaster* arrived in the harbour to show the Allied flag.

Like many large wooden vessels, the *Malahat* hogged and sagged with the waves. But in a quartering sea it gyrated with a double-jointed dexterity that shocked veteran sailors. The decks twisted, contorted and groaned with the strain. Sailors wanting the full effect pressed their faces alongside the deck near the stern and sighted to the forecastle—a full 200 feet—and watched the wave-like undulations.

The end of the war, and the return of steamers to peacetime work, killed the career of many sailing ships. But the *Malahat* survived, thanks largely to the single-minded determination of Carrie Nation to cleanse the US of alcohol. In 1916, Nation's Anti-Saloon League convinced Washington state to go dry. Then, four years later, the country adopted Prohibition. (Canada's provinces had already experimented with prohibition. BC's dry period lasted from late 1917 to 1921, but it was considered a failure—especially by returning soldiers—and repealed.) American Prohibition, or "the great social and economic experiment," as President Herbert Hoover called it, was introduced by the Volstead Act in 1920. It was to last for thirteen years. Thus, with the manufacture and sale of liquor in Canada made legal, and the sale, purchase and consumption of liquor declared illegal in the US, the business of smuggling was set.

And a business it was. Hundreds of men and dozens of ships were employed getting liquor across the border. Some smugglers, like Victoria's Johnny Schnarr and his bullet-like launch *Revuocnav* (that's "Vancouver" backward), worked alone, zipping across Juan de Fuca Strait with cargos of several hundred cases of liquor. Others formed loose syndicates, passing liquor from fish boat to fish boat under cover of darkness. The bulk of smuggled liquor, however, was moved on the so-called mother ships, which rendezvoused at sea with small boats that ran the goods ashore. The *Malahat* became the most notorious mother ship of all.

The mother ships sailed from Vancouver. At city docks, the *Malahat* loaded whiskey, rye, bourbon, scotch, gin, rum, brandy, champagnes, sparking burgundies—as many as 175 different liquors—for a total cargo of sixty thousand cases. Then it steamed or sailed south, peddling its load piecemeal to American smugglers. When the *Malahat* reached the north coast of California it anchored in shallow offshore waters in what was called Rum Row. A favourite position was near the Farallon Islands, where the ship could service the thirsty San Francisco market. The *Malahat* was ideal for this sedate job because it was big and not limited by fuel. It often stayed on Rum Row for a year, replenishing its cargo and supplies from other ships.

Rumrunning sounded glamorous but really was a lot of slogging. Workdays on Rum Row started at 6 a.m. when the ship's wooden decks were scrubbed. (This kept the vessel spotless and prevented the planks from splitting.) The hull had to be kept

clean of growth, too, and the miles of rigging required maintenance. One of the more tedious jobs was bagging liquor. Smugglers discovered that wooden crates were awkward to swing from ship to ship and difficult to store. So they bagged the bottles in burlap, twelve to a sack (which may, incidentally, have led to the peculiar West Coast term for a dozen beer, a sack—or for six, a half sack). A wooden case was opened, each bottle removed and placed in a paper sleeve, then bagged. Sacks had two lugs and could be swung from ship to ship or ship to dock quickly.

Duty and drudgery the seamen could tolerate. Lack of women they couldn't. Lust curdled to loneliness, then to desperation. Rum Row veteran Hugh Garling recalled how, when another rum ship arrived with the mail, the crew scattered into corners to read and reread letters. Others found relief in the crinkled pages of magazines such as *True Romance*. Some of these publications ran ads for singles or, as they were called, lonely hearts clubs. The ads told of shapely, love-starved women, some with large dowries, who sought correspondence with men. Garling remembered that one

sailor sent off his letter, then complained he didn't receive a reply. A prankster on board recognized an opportunity and drafted a reply himself, written in a womanly hand and sealed in an envelope with an authentically rumpled stamp. He slipped the letter into the next mailbag and it was handed to the astonished crewman. The tone was perfect: coy, intelligent and with a whiff of carnality. Thus was born a fervent correspondence. Each mail brought new letters, notching up passions. As the incredulous crewman explained to his barely straightfaced shipmates, he had struck gold. The woman was so friendly they had discussed marriage, and her family owned a pub! The crew kept up the deceit until the ship docked in Vancouver.

Back on Rum Row, the *Malahat*'s sexless, unhurried routine was interrupted by the arrival of smugglers' boats. Fast and sleek, they roared alongside and tied to the *Malahat*'s guestwarp. Then a plank was set between the two vessels and the skipper of the small boat scrambled on board. To make sure a cargo was shipped to trustworthy customers, a system of safety measures was developed. The simplest used dollar bills. Before the *Malahat* left Vancouver, a stack of bills was ripped in two. Half of each bill journeyed with the ship, the others were distributed to accountable customers. Come time for a liquor pickup, the smuggler presented half a bill. If it matched with one on board the *Malahat*, then the crew was given the okay to load.

Loading—the actual swinging of bag after bag of liquor—was assembly-line work. As long as the sea was calm, the transfer was done quickly, interrupted by the occasional crunch of broken bottles in a carelessly thumped sack. The crews bantered about the latest movies or news of the Depression. When the ocean was rough, however, loading was trickier. If a launch was in a hurry, it might try to stand off from the *Malahat* a few feet while sacks were flung from the larger ship to the smaller. Breakage was higher but, relative to profits, still incidental. Otherwise, the ship was loaded the hard way, by piling sacks in a small ship's boat and rowing them through the waves to the launch.

With the arrival of a coast guard cutter, the ship went on alert. First sighting of a cutter was signalled by a holler from the lookout, perched high in the rigging. Technically, the coast guard could not enforce any regulations beyond the 12-mile (19 km) limit, problematically measured as the distance a ship could steam in one hour. In reality, many cutter captains chose to interpret the law as they saw fit. Some were overzealous, others lax. The trick for the *Malahat* was to recognize which skipper

THE THREAT OF A SUDDEN APPEARANCE BY THE COAST GUARD MOTIVATED RUMRUNNERS' CREWS TO WORK FAST. THE BOATS WERE ESPECIALLY VULNERABLE TO BEING CAUGHT WHILE THEY WERE TRANSFERRING SUPPLIES.

was on a boat before it got too close. Friendly cutters were rewarded with a case of liquor, often lowered over the side and marked with a float. Other cutter captains were more straightforward. Garling knew of cutters coming alongside and asking for specific liquors—Jack Daniels, for instance. A case would be set on the deck where it could be reached with the cutter's boat hook. Such losses were written off as contributions to coast guard morale.

Other cutter captains were not so accommodating. They might board a mother ship and, if not actually seize the cargo, then make life uncomfortable. More often they chose to wait a certain distance from a mother ship, knowing that a launch would have to venture out to pick up supplies. Then they would shadow the launch in and, as soon as it crossed into American waters, seize it. A ship hounded closely was said to be "cutterized."

The best strategy was to evade the coast guard altogether. The *Malahat*'s Captain John D. Vosper, a wily, cat-loving Englishman who skippered the vessel for five years, had innumerable ruses. An old time trick of smugglers was to toss booty overboard and fetch it later. The *Malahat* made up a phony parcel of whiskey and heaved it into the water. By the time the coast guard had laboriously retrieved the package, the *Malahat* was a fleck on the distant horizon. A similar ploy was worked at night. The *Malahat* set several torches on makeshift floats configured to match its running lights. With its own running lights extinguished, the ship sailed away, while the coast guard kept a close watch on the decoy. The *Malahat* pulled the trick so many times it became known as the Phantom Ship.

By 1933 it was apparent to even the most zealous temperance leaguer that Prohibition was a sieve. Liquor leached around US borders and bubbled from innumerable underground distilleries. The question was not if the law would be repealed, but when. With the end of the trade looming, the *Malahat* was taken off Rum Row and sold to a Vancouver company that intended to haul logs south from Prince Rupert. The idea was sound, but the owners lacked experience handling the huge timbers. After several futile months upcoast, the ship sailed into Vancouver harbour, its holds

RUMRUNNERS OFF-LOADING LIQUOR FROM THE *MALAHAT*. THE SMUGGLER'S MOTTO WAS, "DON'T NEVER TELL NOBODY NOTHING, NO HOW."

ungraced by logs, its owners too broke to pay wages. It was seized by the deputy marshal. Wage and repair claims totalled $3,800.

It was an indication of how much the marine world had changed that the *Malahat*, built at a cost of $750,000, had trouble fetching several thousand dollars fifteen years later. It was too slow, required a crew of fifteen to twenty-one, and was expensive to insure. Even if a profitable cargo could be obtained, the *Malahat* was limited by the fact that sailors—real sailors, the type who knew a spanker from a Spanish windlass—were dying off. To the many seamen who wandered along the Vancouver dock where the ship was secured, the *Malahat* looked ideal—for a long journey into debt and insolvency. It was teredo fodder.

To a logger family from the West Coast, however, the *Malahat* was an opportunity. For what, he wasn't sure, but then Gordon Gibson had never been a stickler for details. Gibson had not seen the ship, but he knew it was big and strong and cheap—always good qualifications for his type of ventures. If he couldn't put the ship to good use, then it could be stripped and sold piecemeal: the sails were worth $1,000, there was $1,000 worth of fuel in the tanks and the anchor chains would fetch $2,000. The Bolinder engines he could yank out and put to use in one of his family's other ships. The Gibson brothers bought it, sight unseen, for $2,500.

The *Malahat* helped transform the Gibson clan, a beyond-yonder bunch of loggers, into a dynasty. What's more, it did so twice. In 1917, with the family scrambling to stay alive on the West Coast, Gibson's father took a contract to cut ships' hanging knees—right-angled pieces of timber fitted under deck beams in a wooden ship. Gordon and the family laboriously cut L-shaped sections from the roots of trees, working until they had enough for a load to send to a shipyard in Victoria. The money kept them solvent until they got into the more profitable logging business. The knees went into the *Malahat*.

Gibson did not have ideas so much as he had notions. And the notion he had was to use the *Malahat* to transport logs. It was a concept that others, exasperated with losing whole booms in the rough waters off the West Coast, had fiddled with for at least a decade. In 1922 a marine engineer drew a plan for a log-carrying barge, but it was never built. Several years later, Captain Walter Wingate bought the surplus wooden steamer *Bingamon* in Seattle and had Burrard Dry Dock mount a derrick that ran on rails. The ship lugged spruce from the Queen Charlottes to Vancouver, but with mixed success.

The Gibsons, too, had tried a number of ways of moving logs. The most successful was in rafts. Using surplus wire rope, they bound logs into massive cigar-shaped tows. When the raft reached the mill site it was rebound with old hemp rope and the wire stripped off. Then the hemp was soaked in diesel and set afire. As anyone who made the frenzied dash across the exploding raft concluded, there just had to be a better way to move logs.

Gibson thought he had one. He called Captain Vosper out of retirement, and the *Malahat* headed north to the Queen Charlottes for its first load of logs. Off Cape St. James it ran into a gale. The seas were black and huge, the wind pitched to a high

scream. The sails should have been reefed, but the loggers on board didn't know how to work the rigging. Vosper and Gibson became disoriented and lost their bearings. As the ship was swept along—inevitably headed, it seemed, for a rocky shore—Vosper gambled and ordered the vessel snubbed. Both anchors plunged into the water and took hold on the bottom. Though it was travelling fast, the *Malahat* swung about and came to a stop. The canvas took the full force of the storm, but only momentarily. With a detonation like a thunderclap, the belly of every sail blew out.

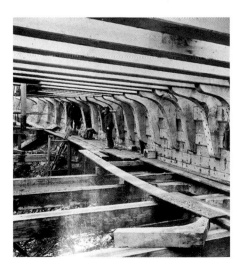

In ten minutes the *Malahat*'s canvas was in tatters. For hours it rode through waves so big that they washed tons of coal from the forward deck and left it piled against the poop deck.

Eventually the storm blew out and the *Malahat* motored to Cumshewa Inlet. En route Gibson set his loggers to modifying the ship with axes and crosscut saws—while Captain Vosper slept. Between-deck beams were hacked out and hatches widened. Despite the alterations, at Cumshewa it was discovered the logs still would not fit. So Gibson, over Vosper's

ABOVE: THE FORMER RUM-RUNNER *MALAHAT* AS A LOG BARGE. AT ONE TIME IT WAS THE ONLY SELF-LOADING, SELF-PROPELLED, SELF-DUMPING LOG BARGE IN THE WORLD.

LEFT: LONG BEFORE THEY OWNED HER, THE GIBSONS CUT THE WOOD AND MADE THE KNEES FOR THE *MALAHAT*.

FORMER TRAWLER-CUM-
STEAM TUG *JAMES
CARRUTHERS*.

pleading, took down the mizzenmast and carved a 50-foot hole in the deck. Then he and his crew built a heavy-lift cargo boom on the spot and began stowing 40-ton logs. Crowned with three 10-foot-diameter logs set lengthwise, the ship carried half a million board feet.

It was all too much for Vosper; he left the *Malahat* after several trips. Then Gibson had a self-propelled log barge (as he grandly called it), but no ticketed master. The ship would have to remain where it was moored, in Esquimalt harbour, until he could find someone with captain's papers. Gibson persuaded Captain Charles Wormald, a veteran of the Canadian Pacific Railway fleet, to try the job. Wormald joined the ship in November 1935. "We drove out to Esquimalt," he later wrote in the *Malahat*'s log. "I hardly knew how to give my impression of the ship which was at anchor in the bay. She was covered with a coating of ice and snow. Everything about her seemed as if it had been under a huge hammer and smashed up. She looked a perfect wreck."

On board, the ship was even worse. Wormald told Gibson he didn't want the job. Gibson, who could be as charming as he could be prickly, said he understood the captain's position. He would take Wormald ashore, he said, but not before giving him a tour of the ship. Gibson's tour led to the captain's quarters. In the room there was a bottle, and a warm stove. While the two were guzzling hot rums below, a mate hoisted the anchor and the *Malahat* steamed out of harbour. It wasn't until the ship was past Race Rocks that Captain Wormald realized the press gang had been at work.

Wormald's shotgun marriage to the *Malahat* was surprisingly successful. If Wormald never approved of Gibson's rough treatment of the ship, he never actually rebelled, either. His position was titular; he was the figurehead to Gibson's dominion. The two sailed the vessel successfully for a year, perfecting the art of moving logs via ship. Log transportation on the coast was changed forever. From the *Malahat* evolved an ever more efficient series of log barges; the post-World War II surplus steel tank carriers; the self-dumping barges developed by Island Tug and Barge in the 1950s; the massive 1970s-era self-propelled barges, such as the *Haida Monarch*, whose 430-foot length could accommodate several loaded *Malahat*s.

Twelve months after it had sailed out of Vancouver to a dubious future, the *Malahat* returned, its decks groaning with a cargo of timber. Seamen gathered to see how Gibson had done it. A reporter scrambled aboard and cornered him and Wormald. Gibson towered above the diminutive skipper. "The Old Man's the feller who's done the trick," he boomed. "He's handled *Malahat* as though she were a tricky baby, humoured her, mastered her, made her go places in these waters. And bad waters they are, make no mistake!

"We pioneered a new industry. And we wouldn't be men if we weren't proud of that. We proved that *Malahat* is a good ship and right for the job. And we've proved ourselves, if you like to put it that way. When she was offered for sale there were men around Port of Vancouver waterfront said we were crazy. They offered the lawyers $2,300 for her, and $2,400, haggling over nickels...I was prepared to buy her, sail her and work her. And we have! She's hard work, but she's fun."

The *Malahat* barged logs for nine years. Until 1937 it was self-propelled; then, after a tail shaft broke, its engines and several masts were removed and it became a hulk pulled behind a towboat. Trailing in the wake of Gibson's steam tug, the *James Carruthers*, it was a familiar sight on the waters between the west coast of Vancouver Island and the sheltered harbours of Victoria and Vancouver.

In March 1944, the *Malahat* was being towed south off Barkley Sound when it began taking water. The barge was towed to Green Bay and the crew removed. While it rode at anchor, shifting logs smashed against the bulwarks, then started the hull's great timbers. They were like battering rams—working from the inside out. Eventually the logs broke free, and the *Malahat*, twenty-seven years old but looking 127, slipped to the bottom.

Lady Alexandra

> Transportation, to be ideal, must have certain aids such as comfort, ease, attendance, a touch of pretension and a good culinary department.
>
> —Aitken Tweedale,
> *North by West in the Sunlight*

If history was trusted to sound instead of to text, the register for the West Coast would include, along with the rattle of boom chains and the slap of salmon on a cannery line, a distinctive ship's whistle: one long, two short, one long. That signal was the trademark of the Union Steamship Company of BC. For seventy years, the Union's black- and red-funnelled steamers bucked bad weather and dangerous waters to supply the logging camps, stump ranches, canneries and mines strewn among the bays and inlets north of Vancouver. The service was oddball, the schedules eccentric. But in their own distinctive way, Union steamers bound the province from north to south as firmly as the steel tracks of the Canadian Pacific Railway bound the nation east to west.

THE *LADY ALEXANDRA* AT SELMA PARK ON THE SUNSHINE COAST. CROWDED DECKS WERE A COMMON SIGHT IN THE DAYS BEFORE STRINGENT PASSENGER REGULATIONS.

Union Steamship was founded in 1889 by John Darling, a director of a shipping line in New Zealand. Darling had arrived in Vancouver a year earlier, via a transcontinental trip on the CPR. His survey of coastal marine transportation started, and ended, in Burrard Inlet. The motley assortment of vessels puffing around the harbour told Darling everything he needed to know about potential competition: there wasn't any. With a group of local investors, Darling purchased or commissioned several small steamers and put them to work serving Pender Harbour, Comox and the mass of timber-rich islands and inlets between Vancouver Island and the mainland, known as "the Jungles." The business was so successful that the Union ships became synonymous with pioneers and loggers. Camps were said to have three crews: one in the woods, one in town, and one on the Union boat. The most famous of these ships was the wooden-hulled *Cassiar*, surely the only ship in BC history that allowed woodsmen to wear caulk boots on board—and even to bed.

Yet there was another side to the Union company. As early as 1889, Darling had spotted a nascent and growing coastal tourism market. Alas, the firm lacked cash to build a swanky tourist boat. As it lamented in a prospectus: "The want of a steamer adapted for this purpose, and excursions amongst the grand scenery... is felt during the summer months."

The company was to feel this "want" for three decades. When they did raise capital, company executives opted to build multipurpose ships to supply the eclectic needs of the upcoast community routes. If and when an excursion cruiser was needed in these years, one of the regular steamers was used. The company promoted the jaunts with the creative explanation that passengers would be enjoying a voyage aboard a "working" ship.

AS A PASSENGER SHIP, THE *LADY ALEX* WAS UNSURPASSED WITH ITS FINE DINING, LIVE MUSIC AND LARGE DANCE FLOOR.

The company grew so much in the war years that its directors felt it could finally get into the tourism business. In 1917 the Union company purchased the assets of the small, Vancouver-based All Red Line. For $117,500 the Union got 7 acres (3 ha) of land south of Sechelt, known as Selma Park, and two steamers, the *Selma* and the *Santa Maria*. These two ships were originally private yachts (the *Selma*, as the *Santa Cecelia*, was built in 1881 for the Marquis of Anglesea or "Mad Marquis," who numbered among his onboard guests King Edward VII and actress Lillian Langtry). Renamed, the *Selma* became the *Chasina*, and the *Santa Maria* the *Chilco*.

The All Red Line purchase was followed by the acquisition, in 1920, of the Terminal Steam Navigation Company. Union Steamship received two steamers, the *Ballena* and the *Bowena*, plus 1,000 acres (400 ha) on Bowen Island, an idyllic setting about one hour's steamer service from Vancouver. The cost: $250,000. Immediately, work was begun to transform the property into a resort, complete with one hundred cottages, a dance pavilion and, in keeping with the company's obsession with things British, a model farm stocked with imported Ayrshire cattle. At the centre of the grounds was an imposing lodge, built in the shade of an even more imposing monkey tree.

To trundle passengers to and from the resort, the company assembled a fleet designed almost exclusively for the day-trip and excursion business. These newly acquired steamers would be ritzier than the Union's usual vessels, and it was decided to give them the "Lady" prefix, to distinguish them from their more utilitarian sisters. (Most travellers knew them as the "Daddy boats," because they brought working fathers to summer resorts on Friday evenings.) Several were conversions, the first being the *Lady Evelyn*, a twenty-two-year-old steamer famous for her rescue work (as the *Deerhound*) in the 1914 *Empress of Ireland* disaster. This addition was followed by the purchase of two former Royal Navy minesweepers, the *Swindon* and the *Barnstable*. Designed for speed, these vessels were made more stable by the addition of sponsons, sausage-like bulges that ran the length of the hull just below the water line. Relaunched, they became the *Lady Cynthia* and the *Lady Cecilia*.

The crown of the excursion fleet was the *Lady Alexandra*. The story of the *Lady Alex* is really the story of an era. During the 1930s the *Alex* catered almost exclusively to Vancouver residents seeking a holiday, a getaway from the sprawl of the city.

(TOP) JOHN DARLING, FOUNDER OF UNION STEAMSHIP COMPANY OF BC.

(BOTTOM) THE MOST FAMOUS OF THE UNION STEAMSHIP'S WORKING VESSELS, THE *CASSIAR*, EQUIPPED WITH AN ONBOARD BAR AND JAIL.

UNION STEAMSHIPS

POPULAR EXCURSIONS

WEDNESDAY, JULY 13

SCENIC 7-HOUR CIRCLE TOUR

around HOWE SOUND

EXCURSION FARE **$1** TICKETS NOW
(Children, 50c) ON SALE

SS. LADY CYNTHIA LEAVES UNION PIER 10:00 A.M.
Returning to Vancouver at 5 p.m.

Lunch on board, 60c. Afternoon Tea, 35c. Music.

SEE "British Columbia at a glance" on this novel circuit of glorious Howe Sound—Vancouver's glorious inland sea. Steamer cruises to the head of the Sound in sight of Mt. Garibaldi through a marine wonderland reminiscent of the Norwegian fjords. No landings made on this matchless vacation trip.

WED. AFTERNOON CRUISE

To SECHELT via BOWEN ISLAND

SS. LADY CECILIA lvs. 2 p.m., and returning lvs. Sechelt 6:30 p.m
(This week.) Return steamers lv. Bowen Wed. 6 and 11 p.m.

FULL ROUND TRIP $1.50   BOWEN ISLAND (return) $1.00

MOONLIGHT Dance Cruise

WEDNESDAY—on SS. Lady Alexandra   Full Round Trip **$1.00**
Lv. 7:30 p.m. Ret., lv. Bowen 11 p.m.   Weds.
Dancing on Steamer and at Bowen Pavilion ....   Only

ONE OF THE BEST ENTER-
TAINMENT DEALS IN
VANCOUVER DURING THE
1930S WAS THE *LADY
ALEXANDRA'S* MOONLIGHT
CRUISE.

They associated the Union company not with double-headed falling axes and fist fights but with the swish of skirts on a dance floor, peals of laughter, and late-night buffets featuring hot drinks and pastries. If such a picture seems a violation of the dominant images of the 1930s—gaunt-eyed rail-riders and Bennett Buggies—then it must be remembered that, even in the worst years of the Depression, 75 to 80 percent of the work force was employed. These people had some money and, if they were fortunate, some holiday time. To them, the Union made an unbeatable offer: round trip to Bowen Island for one dollar—a deal that turned out to be good until World War II. For Vancouverites who could afford that buck, the *Lady Alex*'s rendition of one long, two short, one long, was sweet music.

The *Lady Alex* was built in the winter of 1923–24 by the Coaster Construction Company of Montrose, Scotland. Among its distinguishing features were a promenade deck that ran three-quarters of its 225-foot length, and a polished maple floor extending the breadth of the ship, just over 40 feet. The restaurant, seating eighty-six, was the best equipped of any on the coast.

The *Lady Alex*'s graceful lines always inspired the best in its crew—a hard-case lot of sailors and officers. Even on the voyage from Scotland to Vancouver they were overcome with an unexpected sense of decorum. Instead of taking a direct route from Montrose to the Panama Canal, Captain Charles Barber Smith chose to cruise down the east coast of the British Isles and through the English Channel to Brixham on the Devon coast. Brixham, not coincidentally, was Captain Smith's birthplace. It was said every resident of the town was guided through the ship—twice. After a leisurely one-week layover they departed, setting course for St. Thomas in the Virgin Islands. Halfway through the journey Captain Smith decided he didn't like the wooden boarding protecting the main-deck windows. They made the ship's interior dark and stuffy; outside, it looked hollow-eyed, like Orphan Annie. The boarding was stripped away.

The *Lady Alex* delivered its crew tanned and rested to Vancouver in June 1924. Its first act was to disgorge tons of golden sand, loaded from Scotland's Rossie Island for ballast, onto the beach at Bowen. Then it was shown to the press. The Vancouver

Morning Sun reported: "British mariners have kept the local captains well posted as to the good points of the splendid new steamer and there is hardly a master in the port who is not proud that the *Lady Alexandra* will have her home here."

The *Lady Alex* immediately assumed the role of flagship of the excursion fleet. Whereas other Lady ships showed the inevitable sutures, tucks and stretch marks from their former lives, the *Lady Alex* had pure, clean lines. Other Lady ships were powered by older, cantankerous engines, given to overheating bearings, but the *Lady Alex* was powered by two new reciprocating, triple-expansion engines, capable of propelling the steamer through the water at a snappy 14 knots. It was a magnificent ship. Under a full head of steam, bunting snapping in the wind, there were few other vessels, Union or otherwise, that could match it for stateliness or style.

Within months the *Lady Alex* established that it had a strong personality. Although primarily designed for passengers, the ship also had a large cargo hold. Company officials had hoped that each fall, in the wake of the summer excursion business, the *Lady Alex* might be put to use hauling cases of salmon from upcoast canneries. On its first trip north, however, the *Lady Alex* demonstrated it had no stomach for such work. Returning from the Skeena River, loaded with canned salmon, it hit rough weather in Queen Charlotte Sound. A heavy sea struck the starboard side and the *Lady Alex* listed 35 degrees. Crew slid out of their bunks, caldrons spilled off the galley stove. It staggered back to Vancouver, the crew green of face. The company never let the *Lady Alex* that far north again.

In the role for which it was designed, however, the *Lady Alex* was superb. While the other Lady boats took smaller parties to Howe Sound, Sechelt and Savary Island, the *Lady Alex* whisked hundreds of holidayers to Bowen Island. On special occasions it ran to Victoria, or up the Fraser River to New Westminster. This was the era of the company picnic, and the decks of the *Lady Alex* were often crowded with employee outings for the Hudson's Bay, BC Electric, Kelly Douglas or Woodwards. One of the favourite outings was for Spencer's Remnants, a group of feisty World War I veterans. Twice a week in summer the *Lady Alex* ran moonlight cruises to Bowen Island. The ship rarely rested. In 1937 alone it carried 171,000 passengers.

The decision to put the *Lady Alex* on the Bowen Island run was the brainchild of the Union's general manager, Harold Brown. A slope-shouldered Manxman, Brown came to the Union after working for the Isle of Man Steam Packet Company, whose steamers moved holidayers from Liverpool to Douglas. He was witty and articulate, given to rupturing the sober atmosphere of the Union's offices with bursts of quoted

OLD-COUNTRY WORKMAN-
SHIP COULD BE SEEN
THROUGHOUT THE *LADY
ALEX*, AND WAS ESPECIALLY
EVIDENT IN THE GLORIOUS
DINING ROOM.

Shakespeare. A favourite was from *The Merchant of Venice*: "The man that hath no music in himself,/Nor is not mov'd with concord of sweet sounds...Let no such man be trusted. Mark the music."

In BC, Brown smartly identified a resource the company's literal-minded planners had overlooked: the scenery. With the correct attitude, said Brown, it was possible to see the West Coast as a new Utopia, where the spirits of recreation and physical fitness combined in cedar-scented harmony. Brown began an advertising campaign boosting company ships and resorts. Much of this copy he penned himself. Industrial Howe Sound was recast as a series of "interesting ports of call," including "Britannia Beach, famed copper-mining centre, and Woodfibre, leading pulp and paper mill." Sechelt was located on the suddenly exotic sounding "Gulf Coast Riviera," and Savary Island was declared "one of the loveliest island gems on the North Pacific Coast."

When it came to Bowen Island, Brown went full ahead on the adjectives. It was a "Lovely Isle," a "Happy Isle," a "Wonder Isle"; it was a "Pleasure Garden," a "Marine Playground," a place where the "Spirit of Recreation reigns supreme." Like many well-educated Englishmen—and Fascists—of the day, Brown was infatuated with the therapeutic qualities of volleyball, and many ads featured sexless, sun-browned athletes frisking around a net. Another ad, seen on many Vancouver streetcars, pictured a small boy clutching a toy *Lady Alex*. Underneath, the slogan: Take A Boat to Bowen Island.

Away from the hype, crew found the day-to-day work on the *Lady Alex* extremely hard going. They showed up for work at 7 a.m. to load mail and freight. After a full day of sailing, the ship returned and cargo and mail had to be unloaded. Every day the ship was thoroughly cleaned. Often this took until 7 or 8 p.m. On picnic days and dance cruises, quitting time for the crew would be as late as 1 a.m.—making for a sixteen- or seventeen-hour day. The deck crew were paid $69 per month. Not much, even for the 1930s.

Understandably, staff turnover was high. The quartermaster, winch man and dayman were the only permanent employees. The rest of the deck crew were students and casual labour, hired and laid off depending on the season. Many a Vancouver doctor and lawyer thanked a lousy time aboard the *Lady Alex* for the impetus to carry on with college.

THE *LADY ALEX* AT SNUG COVE, BOWEN ISLAND.

In addition to their regular duties, the crew were expected to maintain order on a ship with up to two thousand partying passengers. Most difficult were the late-night return trips, run from Vancouver to Bowen and back every Wednesday and Saturday. At midnight, the ship's whistle would signal to passengers on shore that it was time to reboard. Then came the rush: throngs of sunburnt, sweaty, tired, happy, lovestruck passengers pushed onto the wharf. As many as five gangplanks were used, and the crush of people was staggering. Standing at the top of the gangplank, pursers and assistant pursers were supposed to take tickets; in reality they grabbed at anything offered. After the ship was loaded, this mess of paper was thrust into the purser's office, to be counted and sorted. Among the items found were BC Electric streetcar transfers and a Chicago hat shop stub.

According to the Union's own brochures, which always reeked of Brown, the *Lady Alex*'s trip from Bowen Island back to Vancouver was supposed to be a pleasant, romantic end to the day. Years later this was the way many passengers recalled the trips. What better place to be than the honey-coloured dance floor of a steamship on a warm summer night? As the ship pulled away, an onboard band would strike up "Aloha" or "At the End of A Perfect Day." In Queen Charlotte Channel music from the band rolled and eddied with the gentle throb of the engines. From the galley came the clink of ice in tumblers and the buttery smell of fresh baking. Couples danced under the stars until the ship passed under Lions Gate Bridge, then crowded shoulder to shoulder against the railings to watch the riot of light emerge from Stanley Park. When the ship finally docked, it seemed as if the Union's dollar ticket had bought them an adventure.

For others, the trip back from Bowen was a chance to get drunk, laid or cause some trouble. Or all three. In the rush of loading, Bowen residents would sneak aboard and when the *Lady Alex* had slipped its lines and was going astern, climb over the ship's bow railing, then dive, fully clothed, and swim back to the wharf. One drunk did a swan dive from the dance-floor railing onto the dining room below. Impassioned couples ducked into nooks and crannies. When Union crews discovered a man and a woman in one of the lifeboats they bolted the covers down and left them until the ship docked in Vancouver. People became sick and vomited, or depressed and cried. One man tried to kill himself. A distraught woman crawled underneath the ship's bridge and refused to leave. One captain had searchlights mounted, and as the *Lady Alex* passed through First Narrows he would turn the lights on and announce through a bullhorn: "Okay, folks, time to end all the lovemaking." Back in Vancouver, crew members had to lug drunks off the ship and stack them, like cordwood, on freight dollies.

Over the years just about every Union master of consequence sailed on the *Lady Alex*: stone-faced Captain John Boden, a former riverboat skipper, who signalled course changes with the tilt of his hat; delicate Captain George Gaisford, with a compass-like sense of direction; popular Captain Roach, who lacked a sense of smell; demure Captain Findlay, who owned his own lead line and sounded every bay on a new route; big Captain Jock Malcolmson, whose chief engineer on the *Lady Rose* hung

BY 1935, BOWEN ISLAND
WAS ONE OF CANADA'S
BEST-KNOWN RESORTS.
THOUSANDS FLOCKED TO IT,
VIA THE *LADY ALEXANDRA*,
EACH SUMMER.

himself in the engine room; and skookum Captain Bob Naughty, famous remover of wharves. None, though, were so intimately related to the *Lady Alex* as Captain Billy Yates.

A small, wiry man, Yates was master of the *Lady Alex* during the 1930s and 1940s. He was a good seaman, his temperament ideally suited to the fun and flash of the excursion trade.

Born in Llanfairechan, north Wales, on May 23, 1889, Yates was indentured at age eleven on board the Royal Navy ship *Indefatigable*. The training ship was manned by misfits or troublemakers turfed off other Royal Navy vessels. Yates was one of several midshipmen, or Snotties, on the ship. These officers-in-training were not permitted to wear shoes on board, lest they slip while working in the rigging. Such conditions inevitably led to runny noses, hence Snotty. (The name may also have come from the fact that these midshipmen had no place to wipe their noses—in fact, buttons were strategically sewn on their jacket cuffs to prevent this.)

With Cappy Yates on board, the *Lady Alex* had the feel of an ocean-going liner. Even in winter, Yates could often be seen on the outer decks, his coat bulging with hot-water bottles he slung from a string and wore front and back. His elfin features were weather worn, and his left ear was damaged by frostbite. Like the best seamen, he could dignify the simplest act. He made the job of lighting his pipe a ceremony worthy of a religious service: first the plank of traditional seaman's hard tobacco was fished from a lint-lined pocket, then a worn jack-knife was produced and the tobacco whittled off. The pipe was tapped clean on the heel of his polished shoe and the tobacco tamped in with a stained finger. Then, with the practised flick of a sailor who has lit smokes in the open ocean, a match was struck and the blaze set. Shipmates who tried the brand claimed it tasted like coal.

Cappy ran a smooth ship. The only problems he had were with Union management. Rightly, they suspected him of being a heavy drinker. It was said among crew members that Cappy Yates could hear a cork coming out of a bottle anywhere on the *Lady Alex*, and get there before the first drops were poured. In their efforts to catch Yates out, Union officials kept a special eye on him, so he couldn't get a bottle on board. Yates got around this by having a faithful quartermaster, who happened to own a windbreaker with deep pockets, make the dash to the Carrall Street liquor store before boarding.

Cappy only came close to getting nabbed once. That was when he was coming back to the Union dock after a particularly boozy trip to open a new wharf at Gibsons. Among those gathered on the dock were several officials, including Eric Suffield, the shore captain known as the "Sea Beast." The Sea Beast had been out to get Cappy for some time. He had a hunch Cappy would be cut. From the dock, it seemed as if Cappy had only two choices: take the boat in himself and risk a crack-up, or stand by while his chief officer did the docking, and face an explanation later. But Cappy was a clever man. Leaving his chief officer inside to dock the ship, he stepped onto the bridge and posed with a second set of controls. The ship slid into the dock like a cork into a bottle.

The relationship between Captain Yates and the *Lady Alex* lasted through the 1930s and 1940s—the heyday of the excursion business. By 1951 the cruise and excursion business was waning, a result of an increasing fascination with the automobile for holiday transportation and an improved highway system. Eventually, the *Alex* was only put into service for the summer months. Then, in 1952, it was withdrawn altogether. Some years later Cappy retired. After sitting in mothballs for seven years the *Lady Alex* was purchased by a group of Vancouver businessmen, and in 1959 the ship was converted into a floating restaurant and moored near the Bayshore Inn. Captain Yates was the guest of honour on opening night. Once a month for several years he journeyed from White Rock for a morning visit to the *Lady Alex*. On

LIKE MANY UNION SKIPPERS, CAPT. BILLY YATES WAS A DEEP-SEA VETERAN.

CAPT. BILLY YATES ON THE
BRIDGE OF THE *LADY
ALEXANDRA*. A FAVOURITE
WITH PASSENGERS BUT
SCORNED BY UNION
STEAMSHIP OFFICIALS,
CAPTAIN YATES WAS A
FIXTURE ON THE *LADY ALEX*
DURING THE 1930S AND
'40S.

February 14, 1966, while cleaning his son's swimming pool, Billy Yates slipped and drowned. He was seventy-six. His funeral notice declined flowers. The staff of the landbound *Lady Alex* asked for and were granted an exception. Apart from the family's flowers at Cappy's funeral, there was one wreath: "From *Lady Alexandra*."

With the floating restaurant business at low tide, the *Lady Alex* was sold in 1970 to another group of local businessmen and sent to the shipyard for remodelling. It emerged a Tahitian-style vessel, renamed the *Princess Louise II*. The Pioneers of the

Canadian Merchant Service Guild declared the remodelled ship an excrescence and expressed "unanimous criticism" at the name change. Norm Hacking, marine editor for the *Province*, said the transformation would make the *Alex*'s designer "roll over in his grave." Outraged seamen did find some comfort in the fact that the opening night for the *Princess Louise II* was a boondoggle. Guests, invited on the ship's maiden voyage across Burrard Inlet to the North Shore, were ordered off by the harbourmaster because life jackets were lacking. The ship slipped across the harbour with its crew, while guests were bussed.

In 1972 the ship was towed from Vancouver to Redondo Beach, California. It was converted to a disco and backgammon parlour, and renamed Dirty Sally's. In February 1980, heavy waves breached a breakwater protecting the vessel and it was smashed against a seawall. Authorities, panicked at the prospect of the old hull breaking up in the harbour, ordered it scuttled in the shallow water at dockside. They hoped the ship would settle on the bottom upright. It didn't. The hull filled with water, then keeled over. Several days later the former *Lady Alexandra*, half-afloat, was towed to sea and allowed to sink. It disappeared in minutes.

MANY SEAMEN WERE DIS-
GUSTED WHEN THE *LADY
ALEX* WAS CONVERTED INTO
A RESTAURANT. THE WORST
WAS STILL TO COME.

BCP No. 45

*A*s a magazine photographer, George Hunter was looking for the elusive combination of light and angle that makes a good shot. What he captured, in a single photo taken in Johnstone Strait in 1958, was the essence of the coastal fishing industry. In the foreground, a white, wooden-hulled seiner worked a set; behind, a fleet of similar vessels bobbed in the water under tumbling coastal mountains. It was beautiful and it was BC. Hunter knew he had a keeper as soon as the image emerged from the darkroom tray. Others who saw the elegant photo thought so, too. The picture enjoyed a decade-long, self-propelled career that saw it splashed across calendars, the cover of the *Star Weekly* and, finally, Canada's five-dollar bill.

THE CLASSIC WOODEN-HULLED SEINER
BCP NO. 45 ON THE FRASER RIVER.

The seiner featured in Hunter's celebrated picture is *BCP No. 45*, sometimes referred to as the West Coast equivalent of Nova Scotia's *Bluenose*, the schooner featured on Canada's dime. (Ardent regionalists say the *Bluenose* is the east coast equivalent of the *BCP No. 45*.) It was built in BC at Vancouver's Burrard Shipyard and manned by BC crews, and it served as a pioneer in the BC seining fleet. In the six decades it worked local waters, it was regarded as a sturdy example of an early wooden West Coast fish boat.

The *BCP No. 45* was one of five table seiners built for BC Packers in 1927. A table seiner featured a roller in the stern that could be turned to ease the task of pulling the net in. The vessels were the latest version of a fishing technology that owed its evolution to the return each year of runs of salmon to coastal rivers. The first fishers, BC's Native people, acknowledged these cycles by designing traps and weirs to catch the salmon heading to the spawning grounds. When they could get iron, they fashioned hooks and trailed them behind their dugouts, a simple form of fishing that later, in its commercial aspect, became known as trolling. Either way, Native fishers took what they needed for food and trade.

Europeans arrived and the survival economy was gradually superseded by a cash economy. Immigrants bought salmon for food and export. By the 1870s, dozens of canneries on the Fraser River were shipping millions of cases to England. Soon industrial demand outstripped the Natives' ability to supply, and other forms of fishing were introduced. Most important were gillnets. Gillnets were slung across rivers much like a curtain across a window. A returning salmon swam into a webbing large enough for the fish's head to pass through, but not its body. Hooked by its gills, the fish could not back away. By the early twentieth century, every major river on the coast had canneries supplied by gillnets. Some of these rivers were also fished with drag seines, a land-based cousin and precursor to the boat or purse seine. Dragnets were set from beaches at the mouths of rivers. The lower edge of the net lay on the

THIS ISSUE OF THE CANADIAN FIVE-DOLLAR BILL EARNED THE VESSEL THE TITLE "THE WEST COAST BLUENOSE."

river bottom; when the ends of the net were dragged in, the fish were hauled in with it. Until 1910, the gill, drag and troll were BC's principal commercial fisheries.

The purse seine differed from the drag seine in that it was set from a boat. Experience and savvy led a captain to a spot where fish—either herring or salmon—were schooling. A skiff towed the end of the net from the seiner's stern in an arc, then reattached it to the mother vessel. The net formed a sleeve, floated by a cork line on the surface and held vertical in the water by a lead line below. A pull on the purse line, which ran from the boat to the bottom of the net, and the sleeve's underwater

end closed, like an inverted drawstring purse. The net and its catch were then dragged aboard. The addition of powered drums to reel in the net—an early 1960s development—reduced the time needed to retrieve a set. With large catches—and sets of almost 1,000 tons have been recorded from seiners—the fish are often pumped out of the seine net, or lifted out with smaller "brailling" nets, and then distributed to several different boats.

Between 1910 and 1920, the seiners joined the troll and gillnet fisheries. When exactly the first boat seine was set in BC is impossible to know. Historian (and former fisher) Alan Haig-Brown suggests the seine fleet was developed rather than invented. Of several isolated events he thought crucial to the genesis of the seine fleet, one was paramount.

This was an experimental fishery conducted for Wallace Brothers' Kildonan Cannery in Barkley Sound, in the years before World War I. According to veteran fisher Charlie Clarke, a steam tug operated by Native skipper Bob Coutes brought a scow into the inlet. On the scow was a seine net. The net was set at daylight, probably using a skiff, and retrieved in the afternoon. The catch was so big the crew used the tug's steam anchor winch to bring it in. Then they gaffed the fish out with cargo hooks—one at a time. When they were finished it was dark. They had filled the scow and five skiffs, and then deck-loaded the tug with 20- to 40-pound (9–18 kg) salmon. In one day they had hauled in enough to keep the local cannery going for three days.

GEORGE HUNTER'S PICTURE OF THE *BCP No. 45* ADORNED CALENDARS AND MAGAZINE PAGES BEFORE BEING REPRODUCED ON THE CANADIAN FIVE-DOLLAR BILL.

The experiment was so successful that the Wallace Brothers leased, then purchased, five seine boats from Washington state the following year.

Canadian fishers tried a number of seine-boat styles: narrow hull, wheelhouse forward, wheelhouse aft. Some designs worked, some didn't. By the time the *BCP No. 45* was built, seiners were of a generally uniform design, embodying the best features for working in the often rough waters of the West Coast. Unlike fish boats throughout the world, the cabin and engine on West Coast seiners were well forward in the hull, with a long shaft extending from the engine through the hull to the stern. The stern was unusually beamy and projected over the underwater section of the hull. The result was a boat with a large stern area above and below decks for equipment, work space and storage, and a hull stable enough to offset the broadside pressures of a laden net. The overhanging stern also helped keep the net from fouling the propeller.

For the first fifteen years of its life the *BCP No. 45* was a company vessel, owned and run by BC Packers or Wallace Canneries. In 1941 it was sold to a thirty-six-year-old Quadra Island Native named Harry Assu. The Assus are a prominent family in the We-Wai-Kai band at Cape Mudge. A tenacious fisher, with happy eyes and a broad forehead, Assu's working life spanned the great years of commercial fishing, when both fish and money were abundant. As a boy he and his brothers lived at water's edge, learning firsthand about fish and fishing. Where there were herring there were coho, they learned. Fish fed at low water slack. When the salmon came close to shore Harry waded in with a club. It wasn't unusual for the twelve-year-old and his brothers to tally thirty good-sized fish in a morning.

While Harry was playing by the water, his father, Chief Billy Assu, and other adults in his village were debating the role, or lack of a role, they and other Natives along the coast were taking in the emerging economy. Would they continue to follow traditional patterns as they had for years, sidestepping new technologies? Or would they take hold of the changes, accept machinery and other devices, and join modern society? It was one of the few crucial decisions Native people were able to make for themselves at the turn of the century. The devastations of smallpox and other introduced diseases were beyond anyone's control. Natives were forced to send their children to school; they were herded onto reserves, which had a way of shifting and shrinking as property values rose. On the water, though, they still governed themselves, much as they had when the *Discovery* and the *Beaver* plied the coast. That life

FISHER LEO DAHLNAS WATCHES AS SALMON ARE BRAILED ONTO THE *BCP No. 45.*

on land would never be the same was obvious even then; life on the water, however, could still go on with at least a semblance of the old ways.

In *Fishing for A Living*, Alan Haig-Brown recounts those early debates:

> Jimmy Hovell, a noted seine skipper from Cape Mudge who retired shortly before his death in the mid-1960s, explained how the decision to adopt modern technology was made. When he was a young man, he, Johnny Dick and Harry Assu's father, Chief Billy Assu, made a trip in the early years of the century, paddling a canoe home from work on the Fraser River. They stopped for the night just north of the present day community of Powell River, at the Salish village of Sliammon. Unlike their home village, this was a missionary village with a sawmill and frame houses in place of the split-cedar longhouses. The men were invited to stay overnight in one of the houses, and they were amazed to see a piano and other powerful symbols of the new white culture in the house. The next day on the long pull across the Strait of Georgia and north toward Quadra Island, they talked about what they had seen. The three young men were eager to try new things, but at the same time they were concerned about the diseases and alcohol brought to their land by the Europeans. When they landed at Cape Mudge, it was with a joint determination to grasp the white man's technology and use it to build a place for their people in the twentieth century.

They started with gas engines. Then came trollers and gillnets. The final move, into seining, was aided by the manipulations of government and the fishing industry. As early as the turn of the century, fishing companies recognized the advantages of pitting the three dominant groups of fishers—whites, Natives and Japanese—against one another. Competition kept prices low and reduced the chances of fishers organizing. In 1922 the government restricted licences for Japanese fishers, and Natives were able to get a foothold in the fishery, first as operators of company-owned boats, then as owners of their own vessels.

Harry Assu bought the *BCP No. 45* in 1941. He fitted it for trolling as well as seining and rebuilt the deck and cabin. For the next seventeen years Harry or his son Mel ran the boat. Those were the best years for seiners. "In those days there were a lot of fish," Assu recalled. "We used to deliver to packers up above Seymour Narrows— we'd deliver every night. I made a lot of money with the *BCP No. 45*."

The day George Hunter took his picture in 1958, the *No. 45* was just off Ripple Point, about 22 nautical miles north of Campbell River. Another Assu boat, the *Bruce Luck*, was in the background. It was owned by Harry's sons Steve and Don. Both boats were doing well. Adams River sockeye, once decimated by a logging dam, were returning in force, and the seine nets bellied with fish. The crew didn't realize their photo had been taken until Mel tossed a copy of the *Star Weekly* on the galley table.

A crewman idly looked at the cover. "Hey!" he exclaimed, "that looks like us!". The picture reappeared on calendars and prints before the image was bought by the Bank of Canada. In December 1972 the bank issued the bill featuring the *BCP No. 45* in the "scenes of Canada" series. (The 1972 bills were replaced in 1986 by the "birds of Canada" series, with a kingfisher engraved on the five-dollar note.)

One of the crew on the *BCP No. 45* during Harry Assu's tenure was future owner Allen "Ole" Chickite. Chickite signed on at age fourteen, as a cook. He was with the boat for eleven years, often working under Mel Assu, Harry's son. "I found Mel Assu to be a very admirable man," said Chickite. "He taught me very well." Chickite skippered the boat during the salmon off-season, fishing for herring in the late 1950s and 1960s. Later, he and the *BCP No. 45* parted, with Chickite taking up gillnetting. In 1984, however, they were reunited. BC Packers, which once again owned the boat, asked Chickite if he wanted to buy it. He said yes, but told the company he did not have any money. "They said, 'Give us a dollar down and make it legal.'" Chickite pulled a dollar bill from his wallet and sailed away.

After replacing the aging table-seine arrangement with a drum, Chickite ran the *BCP No. 45* for several more years. "We had fun, even though there were a lot of trying times out there." The *No. 45* was too small for the heavy drum, but it was still a fine sea boat. "It was built like the old halibut-type boats," said Chickite. "Not narrow, but deep." The ship rolled on a calm day yet was stable in heavy seas.

After five decades of hard fishing, the *No. 45* was still skookum. It took Chickite through four 55-knot blows, and one that registered 60 knots. "I've been through many 40- and 50-mph winds too," he said, "and I sure wouldn't want to go through them again. All we had on there was one radiophone, a chart and a compass—no radar, no sounder. We didn't have the modern gadgets that we do today."

In 1986 Chickite and the *BCP No. 45* spent five weeks at Expo in Vancouver. They took part in the opening ceremonies boat parade, then tied up at the marine plaza.

THE *BCP NO. 45*, BRISTLING WITH THE TYPE OF ELECTRONIC GEAR THAT WASN'T EVEN DREAMED OF WHEN THE SHIP WAS LAUNCHED.

In 1995 Chickite accepted a federal government buy-out offer—part of a controversial and, some say, ill-advised plan to reduce the number of seiners on the coast. Instead of selling the *BCP No. 45*, however, Chickite decided to sell only the licence, and to restore the boat and place it in a museum. "My feelings were she should go back home to where she was built. Let others enjoy it as I have enjoyed it. After twenty-seven, twenty-eight years, you become attached. A boat like that feeds you and clothes you and looks after you; you have some kind of affection." The anchor winch was removed and the forward deck was rebuilt. Chickite chose to donate the *No. 45* to the Vancouver Maritime Museum, in part because it was close to where the boat was built. "I'm kind of a sentimentalist—I think of the Burrard Shipyard and the untold stories of the workers who helped build these vessels. The Burrard Shipyard helped the fishing industry expand."

Chickite made the final run from Quathiaski Cove to Vancouver one night in early 1997. "It was the most beautiful trip I ever made. It was flat calm. There wasn't a ripple. It was a clear, moonlit night. It was 5 a.m. when we arrived and I sort of sneaked into the harbour. It was quiet, just the way I like it."

Minus the bulky drum and net, the seiner was exactly as Chickite had left it after its last fishing trip, including cups on hooks, pots and pans in the galley and jar of Taster's Choice. The wheelhouse clock, stopped in time like the ship itself, registered ten past four. Displayed at the Vancouver Maritime Museum, the *BCP No. 45* is a spectral legacy of the West Coast fishery and the men who worked in it.

OLE CHICKITE IN FRONT OF THE *BCP NO. 45*. HE DONATED THE VESSEL TO THE VANCOUVER MARITIME MUSEUM.

Sudbury

On November 1, 1955, Harold B. Elworthy, the burly, straight-ahead president of Island Tug and Barge, took an urgent cable message at his Victoria office. It was from a marine underwriter in New York. The firm had just heard that one of its client's freighters, the *Makedonia*, was adrift in the North Pacific. The Soviets wouldn't help and the Japanese didn't have a big enough tug. Did ITB want the job?

ISLAND TUG AND BARGE'S FLAGSHIP, THE MIGHTY *SUDBURY*.

It was a question 53-year-old Elworthy had waited a long, long time to hear. In many ways, it could be dated to his childhood afternoons yarding driftwood off the seashore in Victoria's James Bay. Certainly it was traceable to the day in 1925 when Elworthy snapped his briefcase shut and stalked away from a job at BC Salvage. A bright young man, H.B. (which stood, he boasted, for "Hard-Boiled") had learned enough about the towboating business to know he could do better than his former employer, but not so much that he was tradition-bound. He bought a tug called the *Quinitsa*, renamed it the *Island Planet*, and began assembling an empire. The *Island Planet* anchored a fleet of used tugs and gutted wailing ship hulls that horned in on local towing contracts. Like a catch-net snaring flotsam, he bought one towboat company after another: the Gardner family's operation in 1926, Preston-Mann Towing in 1942 and, soon afterward, Commodore Towing. He sold ITB, started Straits Towing, then bought back into ITB. By 1954 his twenty-five-tug, two-hundred-man operation had such a clench on the coastal barge business that newspapers referred to him as BC's "Mr. Towboat."

It was a title that would have satisfied some men, but not Elworthy. Determined to bull ITB into the business of salvage and deep-sea towing, in 1954 he purchased a rakish, war-surplus Royal Canadian Navy corvette-cum-towboat, the *Sudbury*.

The *Sudbury*'s career was as elliptical as Elworthy's was linear. Two hundred feet long, drawing 17 feet, it was built in Kingston, Ontario, in 1941 and commissioned in Montreal. It sailed out of Halifax as a local escort to ocean convoys, then made a trip across the U-boat-infested North Atlantic to Londonderry. Later, it served out of Esquimalt. After the war the corvette was purchased by Pacific Mills and converted into a towboat. Pacific then sold it to an outfit named Badwater Towing, which, like ITB, moved logs and barges.

Badwater set the *Sudbury*, with its huge 2,750-horsepower engines, towing Davis rafts, or giant floating bundles of logs, across Hecate Strait. The venture was only half successful. The ship could pull, there was no question; up to four rafts at a time, eight million board feet of lumber. But such power came at a prohibitive cost: the *Sudbury* was twice the size of a normal tug, required twice the crew and burned four times the fuel. Like Union Steamship's scorned mini-liner "White Boats," also fashioned from war-surplus corvettes, the *Sudbury* was regarded in the maritime community as a colossal flop. Badwater figured they did well to unload the tug to ITB for $500,000.

Elworthy couldn't give a damn what anybody thought. Spending another $200,000, he re-equipped the ship. What had once been navy mess decks were stacked with pumps, air compressors and welding equipment. A fully fitted machine

DESPITE A REPUTATION AS A HARD-DRIVING BUSINESS-MAN, HAROLD ELWORTHY WAS WIDELY RESPECTED BY HIS STAFF. HE BEGAN EACH DAY AT ISLAND TUG AND BARGE BY FEEDING THE BIRDS.

shop included electric lathes, drills and hammers. The bridge was a show room for the latest in radar, loran radio position-fixers, depth sounders and direction finders. Fuel tanks were expanded, crew quarters improved. Even the galley was refitted—as a cafeteria-style kitchen with booth tables. It was like a new ship.

To ITB's competitors, the alterations were money down the bilge. They said Hard-Boiled had become Hair-Brained. Deep-sea salvage jobs were as rare as mermaids; ones that paid decently were even rarer. In the months after the purchase of the *Sudbury*, Elworthy's fast deteriorating reputation was further assailed by the fact that the *Sudbury* remained idle for weeks at a time, quaffing hundreds of dollars a day in wages and fuel so steam could be kept up for quick departure. When the ship did go out, it was to practice at pedestrian jobs, like towing scows, and rack up heavy losses. Behind Elworthy's hulking back, ITB shareholders referred to the *Sudbury* as "the old hog."

But Elworthy never doubted his investment. He justified the money-losing milk runs the *Sudbury* was occasionally sent on as rehearsal time for his crews, so they would all be familiar with the ship when the call came. And to let the shipping world know he was in the salvage business, Elworthy advertised his tug in Lloyd's calendar. Under a big picture of the *Sudbury* was the Elworthyesque declaration, simple and immodest: "The largest and most powerful vessel on the Pacific Coast of North America."

It was this notice that prompted the 1955 cable from the New York underwriters. Elworthy's response: the *Sudbury* would be under way in twenty-four hours.

The story of the *Sudbury* and the *Makedonia* is one of the great rescue sagas of the sea—comparable to the attempted salvage, in 1952, of the Danish freighter *Flying Enterprise* by the British tug *Turmoil*, or the wartime rescues by the *Foundation Franklin*, the North Atlantic tug made famous by Farley Mowat's book, *Grey Seas Under*. For forty harrowing days the *Sudbury* and its charge fought ferocious weather and broken lines. When it was over, the crew were heroes, Elworthy's doubters were vanquished and the *Sudbury*—the war-surplus white elephant—was a legend.

The tale began on October 25, 1955, in Niigata, Japan. On that day the *Makedonia*'s master, the demure, well-coiffed Captain Chrisos Papaliolios received word that the ship was to sail for Victoria, BC. The ship's owner, the sixteen-vessel

THE *SUDBURY* AS A CORVETTE. THE SHIP DID CONVOY ESCORT IN THE NORTH ATLANTIC.

SALVAGE VESSEL SS. SUDBURY
TONNAGE: 892 LENGTH: 204 FT. BREADTH: 33 FT. DEPTH: 137 FT.
Island Tug & Barge Ltd., Victoria and Vancouver

A.G. Pappadakis Company of Greece, had hoped the captain could scrounge a cargo, but despite Papaliolios's best efforts there was nothing. Any further delay and the *Makedonia* risked losing a contract in Victoria, so the owner said go.

Papaliolios obeyed, but reluctantly. The North Pacific kicks up dirty weather in the winter, and the transit would be worse without a ballasting cargo. Furthermore, the ship—a British assembly-line product mass-produced to carry cargo in World War II, and similar to American Liberty and Canadian Park vessels—already had a history of shaft troubles. It was widely known such a problem can be worsened by sailing light.

Papaliolios charted a course that would take his vessel on a great arc along the Kuril Islands north of Japan to the tip of the Kamchatka Peninsula, across the mouth of the Bering Sea, then to Alaska and down the BC coast. At the entrance to the Bering Sea the *Makedonia* ran into filthy weather. When its bow plunged, the stern thrust far out of the water and the prop raced freely. The vibrations set up by this on-again, off-again stress threatened to loosen the ships' rivetted plates, and Captain Papaliolios had been forced to shut the engine down and send out a distress.

In Harold Elworthy's world, great maritime journeys always began with a discussion about money. When he cabled New York to take on the salvage, he offered the underwriter two options for payment. ITB could do the job on "day-rate" and be paid whether the job was successful or not; or alternatively, it could take the job on a "no cure, no pay" basis. "No cure, no pay" meant there wouldn't be any fee if the *Sudbury* failed to save the *Makedonia*, and Elworthy would have to eat the operating

ISLAND TUG AND BARGE BOASTED THAT THE *SUDBURY* WAS EQUIPPED TO HANDLE ANY EMERGENCY. IT WAS FITTED WITH MACHINE SHOP AND DEEP-SEA DIVING GEAR.

costs during the salvage, about $50,000. If, however, the salvage was successful, payment would be decided by a Lloyds of London arbitrator, who would take into account risks, weather, length of tow and other factors. Such settlements often ran to the hundreds of thousands of dollars. An intuitive gambler, Elworthy was delighted when the underwriter chose the "no cure, no pay" option.

Then came the daunting job of readying the *Sudbury*, which was towing a barge upcoast. Elworthy ordered the tug to make for Prince Rupert, drop the barge and take on fuel and supplies. Then he set about tracking the company's top deep-sea master, Harley Blagborne. A slight, soft-voiced man whose hobbies were collecting stamps and coins, Blagborne was a veteran of local and deep-sea boats. He worked for several years on tugs and seiners before going "foreign." Among the ships he had sailed on was the *City of Alberni*, a veteran five-mast topsail schooner bought by H.R. MacMillan, the lumber baron who ran the Crown corporation Wartime Shipping Limited, to freight lumber to South Africa during World War II. Thorough, calm and wise, he was the ideal captain for a salvage mission.

Blagborne was aboard the tug *Island Sovereign*, steaming off Vancouver Island, when Elworthy's orders came through. He hitched a ride into Victoria on a passing fish boat, then flew to Prince Rupert, where the *Sudbury* was fuelled and stocked for the voyage. A glance at the crew list of fifteen told him many of ITB's best men were already on the ship. Both the first and second mates, Roy Blake and Jimmy Talbot, were ticketed tug skippers. Running the engine room was World War II veteran Walter Hitchins-Smith. Even the cook, John Hall, happened to be tops in the ITB fleet. (Hall was renowned for his all-weather cupcakes.) Before leaving Prince Rupert, Blagborne gave each man the opportunity to step down. None took it.

For four days after leaving Prince Rupert the *Sudbury* was slogging north and west, making a steady 13.5 knots. Its course was set for Adak, an obscure port in the Aleutians, where it would refuel before heading in search of the *Makedonia*.

When the ship neared the Aleutian archipelago, the radio operator, Percy Pike, idly monitoring the dial, happened across a drama in the making. A woman on one of the Sanak Islands was suffering complications following childbirth. He radioed the call to the coast guard in Alaska. Then he discovered he was the only radio operator who could hear both parties. For twenty-four hours he relayed messages back and forth. Eventually, Pike arranged for a US Navy plane to evacuate the woman to hospital in Anchorage. Later Pike learned he had saved the woman's life and, out of thankfulness, she had named her son after him.

After refuelling at Adak, the *Sudbury* steamed into the heart of the North Pacific. The seas, which had been calm, now raged. Sixty- and 70-foot (18–21 m) waves thundered onto the decks, smashing gangways and straining equipment. The steel case on a winch was ripped from its mount. There were moments when only the *Sudbury*'s sturdy stack and masts were visible above the froth. Yet always, the tug heaved itself out of the waves and ploughed on.

On November 11 the *Sudbury* received the first clear transmission from the *Makedonia*. This was a pleasant, if puzzling, surprise, since it indicated to Captain

Blagborne that the *Makedonia* was 260 nautical miles closer to North America than it had been when it broke down. When Blagborne first spotted the *Makedonia*, at 1:45 p.m. on November 12, he realized why the ship had shifted position. The crew had torn the tarpaulin covers from the *Makedonia*'s hatches and rigged sails to the masts. The hulking freighter was making a meagre, but critical, 22 nautical miles a day.

Blagborne brought the *Sudbury* alongside, until a mere 100 feet (30 m) of water separated the two ships. He wanted to get a portable radio aboard the *Makedonia*, but the danger of a collision was too great. One touch of the freighter's hull and the smaller vessel's side would be stove in. Nor was there time to await calmer seas. "We weren't in the movies," Blagborne later said, "we were on business. We were being paid to bring the Greek home."

With darkness descending, Blagborne ordered mate Jimmy Talbot to send a line to the *Makedonia*. Talbot was ready. Standing on the tug's heaving deck, he held up a rocket gun, a device that looked like a sawed-off bazooka, took loose aim over the nearby freighter and fired. A rocket blasted out and arced over the ship's bow. From it trailed a fine white clothesline-sized cord that led to a box at Talbot's feet. The cord, hissing smoothly out of its coil, wormed across the water and over the *Makedonia*'s decks. The freighter's crew hauled it in. Four ropes, each of increasing diameter, followed. The last, 4 inches thick, had to be winched aboard. To this rope was attached the *Sudbury*'s towline, a 3-inch cable of high-tensile steel. It, too, was winched in and shackled to the *Makedonia*'s anchor chain. Then the *Sudbury* steamed ahead, paying out line.

Blagborne wanted at least 2,000 feet of line between the two vessels. The towline, weighing 12 tons and hanging far below the surface, acted as a spring between the tug and its oversized tow. Without it, a sudden jerk from the *Makedonia* could rip the great winch from the *Sudbury*'s deck. When Blagborne gave the signal, the winch brake was set and the line momentarily eased tight as the *Sudbury*'s engines strained with the load. Blagborne radioed Elworthy. "We've just hitched up and are coming home." The *Sudbury*, he noted, was already making 6 knots.

After three days of towing, the *Sudbury* was down to 3 knots. Waves pounded over the tug and hammered into the flanks of the high-riding *Makedonia*. Whenever the freighter's bow lifted, the steel towline beat on the *Sudbury*'s afterdeck with such force it could be felt throughout the ship. The crew was never out of earshot of the steel-on-steel banshee.

On board the *Sudbury*, the crew were taxed just to complete everyday tasks. Deckhands checking the winch had to dodge great waves crashing and slopping across the decks, Hitchins-Smith and his engineers clung to handholds to keep from slipping on the engine-room floor. The first rule was safety: if someone was injured, the *Sudbury* would have to abandon the voyage and run for a hospital.

Five days after the *Sudbury* had taken the *Makedonia* in tow, it reached Adak. While the *Sudbury* refuelled, engineers worked on the freighter, attempting to tighten the loose shaft. During this time the crews of the two ships had a chance to meet. Captain Papaliolios invited Blagborne and Hitchins-Smith to dinner. Papaliolios, the

(OPPOSITE) THE CRIPPLED *MAKEDONIA* ASTERN THE *SUDBURY*.

IN HEAVY SEAS, THE METAL-ON-METAL SCREECH OF THE TOWLINE COULD BE HEARD THROUGHOUT THE *SUDBURY*.

towboaters were surprised to discover, lived in relative luxury. Adorning his private sitting room were brocade curtains, fine furniture and tasteful art. The captain greeted them with a diplomat's bow, then offered them cigarettes out of a silver box. After a few introductory remarks, Papaliolios clapped and a steward, clad from head to toe in white, padded in with cocktails in crystal glasses. They might have been dining at an Athenian estate.

Such opulence, Papaliolios explained to the wide-eyed towboaters over dinner of filet mignon and glasses of retsina, was part of business. So was his skill in no less than seven languages and his adroitness at the customs practised in such far-flung ports as Oslo and Zanzibar. Wherever the *Makedonia* journeyed Papaliolios drummed up business by wining and dining shipping agents. Only in Japan had he failed to woo a cargo. And hence, he explained with a careworn shrug, the current troubles.

On Sunday, November 20, the *Sudbury* once again took the *Makedonia* in tow. Makeshift repairs had been carried out on the shaft, and the ship's propeller turned at half speed. For several days the two craft surged along at 9 knots, until huge seas forced Papaliollos to once again shut the engines down. That was at 2 p.m. At five minutes to eight, in zero visibility, the *Sudbury* took a leap forward, knocking several crew members down. Papaliolios's patrician voice squawked over the radio. The *Makedonia*'s anchor chain, to which the *Sudbury*'s towline was shackled, had parted. Thirty fathoms of linkage, weighing one ton a fathom, had clanged off the *Makedonia*'s bows and were trailing at the end of *Sudbury*'s towline.

He may as well have said a torpedo was on its way. A combined total of 42 tons of weight were pulling at *Sudbury*'s stern. With the angle of the towline increasing every moment, there was a real threat of the line fouling the *Sudbury*'s propellor. No prop meant no power, no steerage. Blagborne ordered full ahead on the engines, and at the same time called for the line to be winched in. Inch by inch, the heavy line wound onto the drum, until the first links of the anchor chain clanked over the stern. Mates Talbot and Blake were waiting with hammers. The chain was valuable, but Blagborne was in no mood for saving nickels. "Let 'er go," he bellowed. With a single well-aimed blow, Blake clobbered the connecting pin out of its housing and the chain plunged to the bottom.

In Victoria, Elworthy prowled his suburban home in his pyjamas and awaited the next report from Blagborne. All he knew was that his flagship was in trouble and its booty was adrift. Then the phone rang. Elworthy snatched up the receiver. It was Blagborne. The *Sudbury* had located the drifting *Makedonia* on radar and was tracking it down. The untethered freighter had drifted 130 nautical miles off course during its 46 hours of freedom.

At noon, November 26, the *Sudbury* once again slid alongside the *Makedonia*. This time it took four tries with the rocket gun, but a line was eventually landed and the tow secured. The *Sudbury* had slurped more than 4,000 barrels of bunker oil, double its usual rations over a similar distance. For the next twenty-four hours, the North Pacific hurled its ill-tempered forces at the two ships. Massive seas pounded their hulls. Often the vessels lost sight of each other behind moving mountain ranges of water. Storm followed storm; no one could tell when one gale ended and another began. "Always it was rough weather," Papaliolios recalled later to a newspaper reporter. "Not just rough, but with high seas and winds. I got crazy receiving bulletins—'stormy and gale,' 'gale and stormy,' 'gale warning.' They drive a man crazy."

It was only when the two ships entered the sheltered waters of Dixon Entrance that they escaped the pounding seas. Aboard the *Sudbury*, the crew celebrated a return to familiar waters with yet another round of coffee. Barring a mechanical

THE *MAKEDONIA* IS TOWED
INTO VANCOUVER HARBOUR
AFTER A DRAMATIC FORTY-
DAY SALVAGE OPERATION BY
THE *SUDBURY*, 1955. "NO
SMALLER TUG COULD HAVE
DONE THE JOB," BOASTED
HAROLD ELWORTHY, OWNER
OF THE ENORMOUS VESSEL.

breakdown, the run to Vancouver was going to be straightforward. Aboard the *Makedonia*, however, the confined waters set Captain Papaliolios pacing the bridge. If the towboaters were most comfortable in sight of land, he was most comfortable with open ocean horizons. The mountains and fingering inlets gave him the jitters. His anxiety was even greater when the *Sudbury* towed the *Makedonia* through the restricted confines of Seymour Narrows, where Ripple Rock lurked, a nightmarish hazard to mariners. Though he was technically in command of his ship, Captain Papaliolios wisely chose to accept every one of Blagborne's radioed suggestions. On December 12, after forty wind-racked days, the *Sudbury* towed the limping *Makedonia* into Vancouver and released its charge to a swarm of tooting harbour tugs.

The epic salvage had attracted media attention on five continents, and ITB's office was littered with congratulatory telegrams from marine underwriters and shipping and tugboat companies throughout the world. Elworthy fairly swelled at the attention. "We need only one job a year like this to put us on velvet," he boasted to one reporter. "Why, the *Sudbury*'s nearly paid for herself already. No smaller tug could have done the job."

Several days later, ITB threw its annual Christmas party. According to a contemporary account by McKenzie Porter in *Maclean's* magazine, Elworthy, glowing behind horn-rimmed glasses, was standing in the receiving line when a boy approached. It was an audacious move for a youngster, for the boss was said to have a bite that could sever a towline.

"What is your name, son?" inquired Elworthy.

The boy paused long enough to draw the crowd's attention.

"My name is John Hall," he said loud and clear, "and my dad is cook on the *Sudbury*."

Elworthy gave him an affectionate pat. "Lad," he said, "you have a right to be proud."

With ITB in the starting line-up of international towboating firms, the *Sudbury* rarely lacked work. For years after the *Makedonia* rescue, it kept busy towing scrapped Liberty ships to Japan, then returning with Japanese midsections fitted with false bows and designed to lengthen existing cargo ships in the US. Between these runs there were numerous salvage operations, such as the March 1957 rescue of the *Andros Legend*, a Greek freighter that lost power 1,700 nautical miles off the West Coast, and the December 1959 transport of a disabled US aircraft carrier from Midway to Japan. These and many similar operations did not make headlines, as the *Makedonia* rescue did, but among the maritime community they earned the *Sudbury* a reputation for near infallibility.

By the early 1960s the *Sudbury* had been superceded as ITB's premier tug by a more powerful if slightly less characterful ship, the *Sudbury II*, which ITB bought in Australia. Its boilers worn, the aging original *Sudbury* was sold in 1967 to Victoria's Capital Iron. The wreckers ripped off the tug's decks, then cut away the blunt stern. A crane scooped out its intestines and disgorged them in a dockside heap. Torches were set on the hull. Piece by piece the ship was dismantled until only the keel remained. That, too, was cut apart. Then the *Sudbury* was gone.

VICTORIA TUG HONORED

THE *SUDBURY*'S CAPT. HARLEY BLAGBORNE, FEATURED IN A *VICTORIA DAILY TIMES* ARTICLE ON FEBRUARY 20, 1956.

Pisces I

*U*nder the scudding grey clouds of a December morning in 1966, a small workboat towing a wooden scow laboured out of Burrard Inlet, under the great span of Lions Gate Bridge, and set an unsure northwest course into the Strait of Georgia. The little procession was unremarkable in the context of Vancouver's busy port, with its swarming harbour tugs and hulking freighters, though a few experienced seamen did pause to note the incongruity of the obviously underpowered boat struggling with its cumbersome tow. Probably some gyppo loggers on a rubber-cheque budget. They blew into Vancouver and scoured the harbour of its marine dreck—the paid-off barges, the fire-sale boats—then bulled them upcoast. These seat-of-the-pants mariners, it was said, were either ballsy or brainless. Many thought they were both.

ASSEMBLED IN THE BACK OF A VANCOUVER MUSHROOM WAREHOUSE, THE *PISCES* INCORPORATED HIGH-TECH FEATURES PICKED UP IN CALIFORNIA BY ITS BUILDERS, NICKNAMED THE "T-SHIRT BOYS."

A more colossal incongruity was apparent to the crew of the *Hudson Explorer*, the little workboat leading the parade. As it ground past Point Atkinson and leaned into the long, slow pull to Jervis Inlet, the crew had time to reflect on the magnitude of what they were about to attempt: the first manned deepwater test of their made-in-Vancouver submersible, named the *Pisces I*. If successful, they would hurtle past corporate giants like Grumman, Lockheed and Westinghouse, which were all pitching millions of dollars into the race to build the world's first commercially viable non-military submarine. For twenty-six months, three Vancouver divers, Al Trice, Don Sorte and Mack Thomson, working under the name of International Hydrodynamics Limited (HYCo), had struggled to complete *Pisces I*, a teardrop-shaped submarine now perched on the lumbering scow. They needed to prove the sub could descend to 1,970 feet (600 m) with a pilot. It was this depth that the US Navy had decreed the vessel must be able to achieve if HYCo wanted in on lucrative work recovering sunken torpedoes from the Canadian Forces Maritime Experimental and Test Ranges (CFMETR) at Nanoose Bay on the east coast of Vancouver Island. With the *Pisces* project hopelessly over budget, the torpedo recovery contract was a Holy Grail to HYCo. Complete the test and they could pay down their crippling debt, land other navy contracts and sell their vessel's technology as the most versatile, affordable salvage sub design in the world. Fail to reach 1,970 feet (600 m) and, not only would they fulfill the predictions of all the experts who said the sub would never work, but one of them would very likely be steak tartare at the bottom of the sea and the other two would be commercial diving for the next twenty years to pay off their debts.

In spite of the impressive ring of the name, International Hydrodynamics was anything but a large corporation. It consisted of three partners: the president, who could not spell; the designer, whose idea of research consisted of thumbing through back issues of *Popular Mechanics*; and the general manager, who seriously listed as credentials for building a submarine an incomplete apprenticeship working on wooden hulls at one of the oldest boatyards on the coast. Filling out the staff of HYCo were a deckhand (who moonlighted as a bouncer when paycheques were scarce), a secretary and three poodles.

The three poodles belonged to Don Sorte. Sorte was sometime president of HYCo (in its early days the company did not get tangled up with corporate hierarchies) and chief spokesperson. For this latter task he was admirably gifted. He was 6 feet 2 inches, exotically handsome and fond of attention-getting stunts such as hurling off his toupee while dancing at Vancouver's fabled Cave nightclub. (He kept a table at the Cave, though he did not drink or smoke.) Sorte also loved to flash wads of hundred-dollar bills, which may or may not have had something to do with the non-stop company of impossibly buxom women at his side. If money and spectacle didn't get attention, then his poodles did. Sorte often dyed the dogs different colours (rose, blue and yellow being favourites) and took them out on business, including visits to the service counters of banks. All three dogs answered to the name Tiger. "That way," Sorte once explained in his confident, booming manner, "I had to yell once and all three came."

For all the bravado, however, Sorte was remarkably secretive. His life was sandwiched between an uncertain birthdate, in an uncertain part of the USA, and a mysterious death (or at least disappearance) in 1977, while sailing across the Indian Ocean. In dozens of interviews he never gave the same information twice about his age. (If you take the average of the many birthdates he gave to the Vancouver press during the construction of *Pisces*, Sorte was probably thirty-eight in 1966.)

Sorte had a lifelong love of money, which ultimately—and ironically—led him into the money-gobbling *Pisces* project. This passion may have been the product of a destitute youth. Sorte's dislike of poverty was almost phobic: faced with taking a one-light-bulb room in a cheap hotel or sleeping in his car, he'd choose the car. He was raised in the US Northwest and got a start in business in 1953 by placing what became a controversial ad in a Seattle newspaper. "We will do anything day or night," it said, and was followed by a phone number. He was twenty-five, married with two children and continually short of money.

Sorte was a fan of scuba diving, which in the 1950s was still in its infancy. He was attracted to the frontier aspects of diving and soon realized it was a potential moneymaker. He took a miscellany of underwater jobs, including a regular gig recovering accident victims from submerged automobiles. The police, all too aware of Sorte's immoral imperatives, advised him to stay out of the victims' pockets; they needed the wallets for identification.

With no training or experience, Sorte took on contracts to salvage sunken logs from freshwater booming grounds. His approach was simple. With a heavy set of tongs attached to a crane, he rowed or waded into the water and slammed the tongs into a log. The crane then pulled the log onto land. The water, of course, quickly filled with sludge and goop dragged from the bottom, so he worked by feel, slithering over piles of slime-covered logs. If the pile shifted, he could be trapped or crushed. It was a lucrative business, though, and lasted until Sorte broke up with his wife and moved to Vancouver with a new girlfriend.

Sorte's chance to break into the closed shop of the BC commercial diving scene came in June 1958, when a span of the Second Narrows Bridge collapsed, killing eighteen workers. During attempts to recover bodies trapped in the wreckage, a commercial diver was lost as well when he was carried off by the tidal rip. Whether or not it was because of the accident (Sorte felt it was), the divers' union opened its doors a crack and he was inducted into the brotherhood of Local 2404 of the Pile Drivers, Bridge, Dock and Wharf Builders of Vancouver, as a commercial diver.

Sorte became an excellent diver and was paid well, but the work could be dangerous. During one job, a supposedly routine hard-hat chore cleaning up under a Vancouver pier, his air supply was accidentally cut off. The intake hose from the compressor, always placed upwind and well away from the exhaust fumes of the motor, had been left hanging near the surface of the water. Spray was sucked into the hose by the compressor and shunted down into the helmet. Don immediately closed the air hose control valve. No water was going to get in, but neither was any air.

"They tell you there is a five-minute air supply inside your helmet, but I find you tend to black out after three minutes," Sorte recalled. "I began gathering up all my hoses and such to move out where I would be clear to be drawn up by my tender. I kept calling out to him on my voice line, 'George, are you up there? George! Where are you, George?'"

George was away momentarily, getting coffee.

Sorte regained consciousness flat on his back on the wharf with George slapping his face and crying at him to wake up.

With his diving earnings Sorte bought a home, complete with pool, in the tony British Properties district of West Vancouver. He cruised town in flashy cars. He even had an oil painting commissioned: it portrayed a man kneeling in adoration before a huge dollar bill. "One thing about Sorgee," a friend explained. "You didn't take him seriously, you just experienced him."

Sorte met Al Trice through his diving work. Trice, a soft-spoken, pipe-smoking Steve McQueen look-alike, was an early member of the divers' union and a long-time regular in Vancouver's waterfront community. After a brief attempt, in his teens, to manufacture wooden sailboats, he drifted through a variety of maritime jobs: fish boat deckhand, towboat skipper and, finally, apprentice shipwright at the venerable Star Shipyard (Mercer's) Limited in Queensborough, near New Westminster. "Everything was big: the hammers, the chisels, the planes—everything," Trice recalled. "They used to say, 'If it isn't hard work, it isn't Mercer's.'"

The yard was not graced by anything that might be called technology. There were no cranes. It took three weeks to put a 2-ton engine in a boat. As Trice explained, "Together with your helper—just one, you always had just one helper—you wedged it up, built a bridge across the deck of the boat, levered it over, then eased it down into the engine room. Scared to death the whole time the thing would get away on you. It was like building the pyramids."

All this was conducted under the eye of Mercers' temperamental foreman. "If you're going to smoke," he once declared to Trice, "you're going to smoke tailor-made. You're not rolling on my time."

In May 1953, Trice met Keith Carter, an ex-British-Navy frogman. Within a week Carter took Trice diving and Trice was hooked. This, he knew, was his calling. Trice especially enjoyed the three-dimensional freedom of diving—where "up" and "down" lost meaning. He and Carter formed a business, hoping to promote scuba as

DIVERS DON SORTE AND AL TRICE WERE CONVINCED THEY COULD BUILD AND PROFITABLY OPERATE A SUBMERSIBLE.

an alternative to the more prevalent hard-hat diving. But hard-hat divers were unimpressed with scuba. They referred to the aqualung as "mouse gear" and the divers who used it as "frogs." Trice's attempts to sell Vancouver on the merits of the new diving technology failed, and the business folded. But his diving career flourished. By 1964 Trice was one of the most respected commercial divers in the Lower Mainland. That year he was called on to make some of the riskiest dives of his life.

In early spring of 1964, *Barge 10*, loaded with heavy bunker oil, turned turtle in heavy seas and sank near Pasley Island in Howe Sound. Trice was asked to do the salvage survey. Compounding the usual dangers was the fact that Trice would be diving alone to depths of at least 250 feet (80 m). Jacques Cousteau, the French underwater pioneer who popularized scuba diving, had stated in a book published in 1963 that 200 feet (61 m) was the maximum depth for "aqualungers," as he called them. Divers were still using ordinary air, which is 79 percent nitrogen. (Nitrogen gas enters the bloodstream under pressure and is responsible for the crippling, sometimes fatal bends divers can get when they surface too quickly.) "You did lots of dives to 80 metres alone," said Trice. "They wouldn't pay for two divers. That's all there was to it. Some dives you just have to back out of. You just can't do that dive. You'd get too narc'd."

"Narc'd" refers to the other problem dissolved nitrogen causes: nitrogen narcosis, the effects of which are often quoted in martini equivalents. For each 66 feet (20 m) a diver descends, the amount of nitrogen forced into the bloodstream by the increasing atmospheric pressure has an impact roughly equal to drinking one martini. At 330 feet (100 m), or after pounding down five quick martinis, a diver's thought processes become confused. He does foolish things, like offering his aqualung to passing fish or remaining on the bottom long after his dwindling air supply should have sent him back to the surface.

Working alone, Trice completed his survey of the wreck. He discovered *Barge 10* was leaking. In his report he noted the barge lay on a slope with its shallow end at a depth of 260 feet (80 m) and the deep end at 330 feet (100 m). Even at 260 feet (80 m), each minute a diver spends on the bottom requires a corresponding amount of decompression time at various stops while returning to the surface. At 330 feet (100 m), the decompression time would be dramatically increased. The problem was going to be air supply: a diver needed enough to descend, work, then make the long, slow ascent.

Trice, Sorte and another diver were contracted to do the underwater work. It was to be the deepest diver salvage operation ever undertaken, hard-hat or scuba—anywhere on the west coast. Prior to the work on *Barge 10*, Trice and Sorte had been to such depths only a few times, on sporting test dives off Vancouver's North Shore. The men had done a so-called "bounce" dive, going down to 330 feet (100 m) and straight back up. (Years later a good friend of Trice's drifted to the surface dead after a much shallower bounce dive.)

The underwater work on *Barge 10* proved more difficult than Trice or Sorte had anticipated. After several twenty-five-minute dives at the work site, they had to reduce bottom time to fourteen minutes per dive. Fourteen minutes was just enough time to secure a shackle or work a pin into place. Then it was time to make for the surface, following a carefully planned schedule. On the support ship they scrambled out of oil-coated suits and into a decompression chamber, where they often slept for hours. They shortened their work schedule to four days on and three off, and still they were exhausted.

The *Barge 10* job was successful, but it convinced Sorte and Trice that they needed a submarine. Just as the aqualung freed the hard-hat diver from his awkward gear, so a submarine would free the diver from all the hazards associated with working at extreme depths. A sub would double or even triple the diver's range of operations. The men's ideas were fuelled by the fact that Cousteau's submarine *Denise* (or "Diving Saucer," as she was also known) and her surface support ship *Calypso* were in operation off the coast of California in early 1964, receiving a lot of media and trade-journal coverage.

One morning shortly after the salvage of *Barge 10*, Trice appeared in front of Sorte's posh West Vancouver home and announced he was heading south to look at submarines. Sorte didn't even pause. He shot inside, crammed a toothbrush in one pocket and a bulging wallet in another, and the two headed off on an unusual shopping trip.

In California, Trice and Sorte visited corporate giants Westinghouse Electric, General Dynamics and General Mills, which were all working on submersibles, and in every case they were welcomed more as colleagues than as potential competitors. Executives began calling the Canadians "the T-shirt boys" because of their casual attire. Despite, or perhaps because of, their unprofessional appearance, Trice and Sorte were ushered into the deepest recesses of the security-conscious research laboratories. (At Lockheed's aerospace research centre they were allowed to watch a prototype moon buggy being put to the test.) Although boggled by the technological excesses of the American submersible programs, Trice and Sorte did note many practical features, including portability. To be useful, a submersible had to transport easily—in aircraft or on ships and barges.

The *Pisces* was eminently portable. On that December day in 1966, the *Hudson Explorer* and its tow entered the deep waters near Captain Island in Jervis Inlet, the submersible lay on the flat expanse of the scow's deck like an avant-garde table ornament. As Sorte and Trice brought the *Explorer* alongside the barge, HYCo's third partner, Mack Thomson, got ready to dive. Unlike hard-hat or scuba diving, work in a submersible requires no special gear. For the occasion, Thomson, 5 feet 8 inches and 135 pounds, had troubled to don his favourite James Bond 007 sweatshirt. The *Pisces* didn't require a lot of preparation, either: its batteries were charged, its oxygen tanks filled. The only thing that distinguished this dive from many others—besides the extraordinary depth—was the web of stress wires stretching across the submersible's crew chamber. These wires spotted microscopic shifts in the sphere's dimensions by measuring changes in the wires' electrical resistance. For Thomson, this was an unusual concession to technology. Ever making do, he had tested the hull of the *Pisces* in its first unmanned submersions by lashing pieces of wooden lath together. If the sphere contracted while submerged, the laths slid past one another and Thomson was able to measure the difference when the craft returned to the surface. To date, the *Pisces* had exceeded everyone's expectations.

Moving with practised ease, Thomson clambered into the *Pisces*'s crew chamber and secured the hatch. Outside, the cable from the scow's on-deck crane was hooked to the submersible and it was hoisted over the side. The descent to 1,970 feet (600 m) was scheduled to take several hours. Without complicated decompression stages to go through, the craft would simply drift down to the designated depth; then, after blowing water ballast with compressed air, it would return to the surface.

Prior to building the *Pisces*, Mack Thomson's closest formal contact with submarines had been the Wednesday-evening meetings of the Seattle contingent of the US Submarine Naval Reserves. He had joined the reserves not because he was fascinated by submarines—he was more interested in boats—but because it was an alternative to being drafted for two years of military service. In his four years with the reserves, he never once went down in a submarine. Sea duty consisted of a few cruises in small navy ships on Seattle's Lake Union, during which Thomson was occasionally allowed a turn at the helm. He was told to "steady up on Grandma's Cookies"—a large billboard at the head of the bay. The assignment that carried the greatest burden of responsibility was to teach knot-tying to a junior class. As soon as his obligatory time was up, he resigned.

Thomson was a nudist, and a spiritual brother to Zen mechanic Robert Pirsig in the sense that he had a near-spiritual affinity for matters technical. "Mack sometimes thinks something, and then, to him, it is," said Trice. "He doesn't differentiate."

Like Sorte and Trice, Thomson first got into scuba diving as a sport. Too broke to buy a dry suit, he made his own rudimentary outfit by gluing and stitching together yards of the material used to protect baby mattresses. By wearing a full set of woollen long johns under this plastic suit, he was able to tolerate the frigid waters of Puget Sound. He acquired a secondhand regulator, then made his own K-valve to fit the breathing apparatus to his air tank.

Thomson's inventiveness blossomed in the frontier world of scuba diving. Using salvaged parts, he manufactured an underwater lighting system that, for the first time, enabled photographs to be taken at depths of greater than 33 feet (10 m), the approximate limit for full-spectrum light. He showed some of his photos to Don McKuen of KOMO-TV, who hosted a popular program called "Exploration Northwest." McKuen was so taken by the photos, and by Thomson's contagious enthusiasm, that he teamed up with the diver to produce several programs, one of which garnered the station a prestigious Sylvania Award. Occasionally inventive beyond recklessness, Thomson once thought he had found a nifty way to ascend from the depths by blowing up his suit like a balloon and rocketing to the surface. A horrendous case of the bends arrested further development of that idea.

Thomson was the kind of guy who read technical and trade magazines. In one of these journals he came across an account of how Washington's Grand Coulee Dam

AL TRICE IN THE
UNFINISHED MAIN SPHERE
OF THE *PISCES*.

was regularly inspected by hard-hat divers. It was risky work. The dam is one of the largest in the world—the waterfall over its spillway is 350 feet (107 m) wide and falls more than 160 feet (50 m)—and the terrific currents in and around the areas to be inspected were extremely hard on divers in their cumbersome gear.

Thomson concocted the idea of doing the inspections in modified scuba gear and immediately focussed all his exuberance on a drive to convince fellow divers it could be done. Instead of the bulky hard-hat suits, they would use seamless wet suits, made in typical Thomson style by pouring rubber over manikins. Each diver would wear a small tank of air for emergencies. Connecting them to the surface would be air hoses, and telephone and safety lines. With the increased mobility, Thomson reasoned, they could do the inspections much more quickly and much more cheaply than hard-hat divers.

Thomson's bid on the job was successful. The inspection was done in September, when the water level in the dam was as low as possible. The giant turbines were slowed to a minimum, and the divers went to work. The water was absolutely clear, so much so that Thomson, working from a platform halfway down the inside of the dam, had an attack of vertigo. He felt he would tumble through the water to the bottom.

Thomson met Sorte and Trice in Seattle in 1964, at the home of a mutual friend. Trice and Sorte were on the way home from their shopping trip, unimpressed by what they had seen. Two other manufacturers, American Submarine Company of Ohio and Perry Submarine Builders of Florida, had both built subs that could dive to 100 feet (30 m), but neither was designed for salvage work. Even when they looked beyond North America, the only other sub remotely close to their needs was Cousteau's *Denise*, completed in 1959. A prototype, it was described as "a scrutinizer, a loiterer, a deliberator, a taster of little scenes as well as big," but it was not on the market.

The remaining option was to build a sub, but that too sounded unfeasible. Before leaving Vancouver, Trice had run the idea of building a sub by an engineer at Patterson Boiler Works. "The man was very nice. He sat down with us and carefully explained why building a submersible was impossible." Despondent, Sorte and Trice asked Thomson if he could build them a sub. Thomson said yes.

His first step in the design of the sub was to inhale as much of the literature as possible. Among the many texts Thomson consumed was the account of a Swiss man named Jacques Piccard, one of the foremost authorities on submersible design at that time. In 1960, four years before Thomson started on his sub, Piccard, backed by the French Navy, had reached a depth of 6 nautical miles in a submersible named the *Trieste*. The dive, which set a record that still stands, was made in the south Pacific Ocean, in a trench named the Challenger Deep. The overall design of the *Trieste*, which employed an enormous bag of gasoline to lift the sub to the surface, was totally impractical for a salvage sub, but Piccard's account was invaluable. In particular, Thomson noted Piccard's advice that "the cabin is the vital part of any deep ship; around it all other components must be fashioned." A submersible's cabin must be capable of withstanding tremendous pressures, while keeping its crew not only dry but at the same atmospheric pressure they left at the surface. The pressure on every square inch (6.5 cm²) of the cabin's outside surface increases at a rate of almost 1.5 pounds (660 g) per 3.3 feet (1 m) of depth. At a depth of 3,300 feet (1 km), the pressure is over 1,460 pounds (660 kg) per square inch (6.5 cm²).

The hull design with the smallest surface area—or the shape that mathematically optimizes the weight-displacement ratio and distributes the pressure most evenly over the surface—is a sphere. Otis Barton's bathysphere, in which he and William Beebe were lowered on a tether to an ocean depth of 3,050 feet (930 m) in 1934, was about 5 feet (1.5 m) in diameter, which gave them space enough to see if they could do it but too little space to provide a working environment for a salvage job. Thomson knew his sub would need room for a crew of two plus masses of equipment.

When asked where he had got his information about hull design and materials, Thomson explained: "We just ask our friends. We've got lots of friends who give us information." One of those friends was Warren Joslyn, one of Boeing Aircraft's top stress engineers. Joslyn's original contribution to the project was the terse comment that it was impossible. Then, snared by Thomson's limitless enthusiasm (as many,

DESPITE BEING OVER BUDGET AND BEHIND SCHEDULE, THE THREE INTERNATIONAL HYDRODYNAMICS LIMITED (HYCO) PRINCIPALS FOUND REASON TO CELEBRATE THE COMPLETION OF THE *PISCES'* SPHERES. LEFT TO RIGHT: AL TRICE, MACK THOMSON, DON SORTE.

many others would be), he began designing. The engineering specs he prepared for Thomson called for the submersible to be built around two spheres, a larger one for the crew and a smaller one containing various tanks. It would be capable of submersion to 1,640 feet (500 m). Vancouver Iron and Engineering contracted to build the spheres. Thomson took office space in their shop, and the long job of bending metal began in the summer of 1964. After six months of relentless work, the frame and two spheres were completed. The bill was almost $50,000, thus cleaning out HYCo's entire budget. (The US Navy had paid $50,000 for a submersible named the *Intelligent Whale* in 1872!) HYCo moved the *Pisces* from the fabricators to an unused space in the back of a mushroom cannery in east Vancouver. They secured the space in return for helping load crates of tinned mushrooms onto trucks. Power, steering and breathing systems were completed, but slowly, as Thomson often worked without benefit of engineering drawings. (Incredibly, the *Pisces I* was built from a total of forty-four drawings, about the same number, an engineer claimed, needed to construct a coat

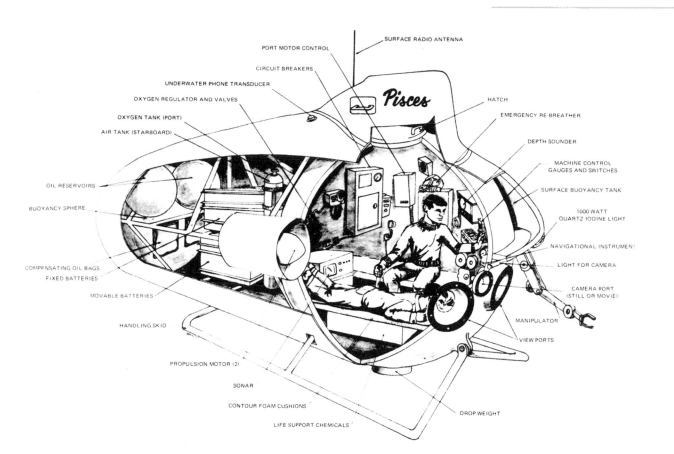

SURFACE RADIO ANTENNA

PORT MOTOR CONTROL

CIRCUIT BREAKERS

UNDERWATER PHONE TRANSDUCER

OXYGEN REGULATOR AND VALVES

OXYGEN TANK (PORT)

AIR TANK (STARBOARD)

OIL RESERVOIRS

BUOYANCY SPHERE

COMPENSATING OIL BAGS
FIXED BATTERIES

MOVABLE BATTERIES

HANDLING SKID

PROPULSION MOTOR (2)

SONAR

CONTOUR FOAM CUSHIONS

LIFE SUPPORT CHEMICALS

HATCH

EMERGENCY RE BREATHER

DEPTH SOUNDER

MACHINE CONTROL
GAUGES AND SWITCHES

SURFACE BUOYANCY TANK

1000 WATT
QUARTZ IODINE LIGHT

NAVIGATIONAL INSTRUMENT

LIGHT FOR CAMERA

CAMERA PORT
(STILL OR MOVIE)

MANIPULATOR

VIEW PORTS

DROP WEIGHT

hanger.) Thomson built many parts himself, often at home in the evening. The next day he would show his handiwork to Trice, who would find a way to drop it on the warehouse floor. If the part broke it wasn't any good; if it survived, it had passed the *Pisces* quality test.

Originally, HYCo's partners had hoped for the sub to be ready in three months (and for $20,000). After fifteen months, Trice and Sorte, in the depths of debt, insisted on seeing the sub tested in the water. Thomson, who had an inventor's disregard for time and budget, said he wasn't quite ready. They would have to wait. By this time the *Pisces* had been moved into a little shack at the end of Vancouver Pile Driving's pier in North Vancouver. Desperate to see how their investment was going to perform, Trice and Sorte waited until Thomson was away, ran the *Pisces* out on the I-beam and lowered her into the ocean. The submersible did not float level at all; the tail end sank. Sorte, who was never big on reining in his emotions, developed a case of the financial bends, declaring in dismay that the whole venture had been an enormous waste.

When Thomson returned, they confronted him with the sub's problem. Thomson was typically philosophical. "Oh, well," he said. "We learned a lot." This sent Sorte into even greater paroxysms of anger and frustration. He had been taking every diving job that came along in order to finance the sub, and it wouldn't even float straight. It fell to Trice to defuse the situation. "What are we going to do?" he deadpanned. "I

AMPLE CREW SPACE WAS A PRIORITY IN THE DESIGN OF THE *PISCES*.

don't know. Give up." Disgusted, Sorte and Thomson agreed to carry on.

"There's no magic," said Trice, who had an engineer's patience for mechanical problems. "You can only use what's there. We're always asking for magic. There is no magic."

The problem of the *Pisces'* heavy tail proved easy to solve. Thomson bought two hundred Grimsby troll floats at a nearby commercial fishing store and crammed them into every accessible tail section of the *Pisces'* fairing. Each float had 6.6 pounds (3 kg) of lift and was good to a depth of no less than 1,725 feet (525 m).

Among other problems plaguing the emerging submersible was arc and fire—or, in HYCo lingo, "A & F"—in the electrical system. Electrical problems became so common they were spoken of lightheartedly, but shadowing the jokes was the memory of a fire of catastrophic consequences on board one of Jacques Cousteau's test subs, caused by a short. The sub was quickly lifted onto the deck of the *Calypso*, but when the fire couldn't be put out with carbon dioxide foam it was dropped back into the sea. If there was a bad fire in the *Pisces* while Thomson was aboard, even alongside the docks, there was no one to yard the sub out of the water quickly. Testing was a serious business.

Thomson often worked on the *Pisces'* interior while it was submerged off VPD's dock. With a radio blasting, he painted the hull aquamarine and white, then set to installing an infinity of controls. The chronic shortage of money led to continual compromises. For example, the scrubbers that controlled the critical level of carbon dioxide in the air were driven by a sewing machine motor. Thomson had lifted it from his wife's Singer during a conjugal visit to Seattle. He did splurge on a telephone, which he hooked up inside the *Pisces* to save himself the bother of having to clamber in and out whenever he needed to call for parts or advice. People on the other end of the line, listening to Thomson's echoing voice, jokingly asked if he was inside a well. He replied that he was sitting at the bottom of Burrard Inlet.

In the mountainous confines of Jervis Inlet, the crew would need more than a phone line to stay in touch with Thomson, particularly at the depths he intended to reach during the dive. Underwater communication equipment was only marginally effective in those days. Radio waves could not be used, as they spread out rapidly in water and soon became unintelligible. The *Pisces'* communication system was based on sound. Sound can travel for hundreds of miles in water if conditions are right, but refraction can be a problem; sometimes the sound bends as it travels. As the effects of refraction are minimized on the vertical plane, it was imperative the *Explorer* sit directly above the *Pisces*.

Complicating the problems of communication was the proximity of a US Navy vessel, also in Jervis Inlet. After contacting the ship—an innocuous-looking buoy tender—the crew of the *Hudson Explorer* were alarmed to discover it was testing a new generation of antisubmarine torpedo. These were being fired out a tube on the stern of the ship, then whizzing away in search of underwater targets.

Thomson irreverently radioed the US ship, explained what HYCo was about to do and asked it to postpone torpedo tests. The Americans, working to schedule, were reluctant to cancel their tests but stopped just short of refusing. They may have recalled an incident that had occurred before the testing of the US submersible *Deepstar 4000*. Its support boat was mistaken for a target by a navy ship and had three 5-inch (13-cm) projectiles dropped 660 feet (200 m) astern of it before the crew were able to advise the navy of its error.

THE *PISCES* SUSPENDED FROM VANCOUVER PILE DRIVING'S PIER IN NORTH VANCOUVER.

MACK THOMSON PREPARES
FOR THE *PISCES* DIVE IN
JERVIS INLET.

The HYCo team and the US Navy ship established what they considered to be a reasonably safe distance between them. It was also agreed the navy would advise HYCo when they were about to fire a torpedo by raising a red flag. This signal was a near-useless concession, as the torpedoes were fired from the deck of the ship: the HYCo crew could watch the launches through binoculars.

During what was supposed to be a long break in the torpedo tests, the *Pisces* began its descent. Crouched below the stress wires, Thomson guided the vessel under the surface as easily as he would back his car out of the garage. By this time the fantastic and foreign treats of underwater travel were familiar to him. To the few guests who had been down in the *Pisces*, even to relatively shallow depths, it was like a trip to a new world. One US fisheries expert, a guest on a dive in Puget Sound, had taken along a tape recorder and a camera. So dazzled was he by the first-time sight of the rich waters that, as Thomson gleefully noted, he spent much of his time talking into his camera's light meter and pointing his microphone out the view port.

Thomson's first checkpoint was at 560 feet (170 m). He reported all was well, although the response from the *Hudson Explorer* was garbled. On the surface, the crew of the *Explorer* were having equal difficulty understanding Thomson's scratchy reports. To Trice, the communication problem hinted at a more serious situation. He realized they were no longer directly above the sub; the *Pisces* had drifted out from under them—and toward the torpedo target. As Thomson continued with his descent someone on board the *Explorer* noticed a red flag raised on the navy boat. There was no time to call off the dive. Warren Joslyn, along for the ride, tried frantically to advise the navy to hold fire, but the Americans suddenly seemed to develop communication problems of their own. Trice advised Thomson to shut everything off aboard the *Pisces*. Then, with gut-wrenching horror, the crew of the *Hudson Explorer* watched a torpedo shoot from the deck of the navy ship, splash into the water and hurtle away.

Far below, Thomson had been recording his thoughts and observations on a tape recorder. He had heard enough of the squawking message from the *Hudson Explorer* to realize his predicament. He shut down all unessential electrical gear. The *Pisces* was now still and silent. Thomson even clapped his hand over his wristwatch to muffle its ticking. He left the tape recorder running, and on the tape one can distinctly hear the whine of the torpedo's screws as it cut through the water seeking a target. Thomson heard it too, of course, crouched in the sub, alone, 660 feet (200 m) underwater, waiting for any change in tone to indicate the torpedo had homed in on the *Pisces*. Even though the torpedo was unarmed, he knew it was a tossup whether it would impale the *Pisces* or pass right through.

After an unbearably long time, the sound of the torpedo trailed off and Thomson continued the dive. When he paused at 1,080 feet (330 m) to take stress readings, there seemed no particular problem other than the discovery that he had lost all communication with the surface. Normally, this would have been cause to call off the dive, but after the business with the torpedo the loss of communication didn't seem that serious to Thomson. Besides, HYCo didn't do things normally.

Shortly after the *Pisces* passed the 1,310-foot (400 m) mark, an explosion jarred Thomson from the controls and the sub plunged downward. His first reaction was to leap up, thus becoming snarled in the stress wires. Fighting to free himself, he struggled with the controls to blow the ballast tanks and arrest the descent. There was the familiar hiss of compressed air and gurgle of bubbles as the tanks were cleared, but the *Pisces* did not respond. It continued to sink. Thomson could see particles like dust motes, illuminated by the 1,000-watt headlights, snowing upward outside the viewing ports.

Down the *Pisces* went, level but uncontrolled, like a feather wafting from a nest. While the depth gauge recorded his plunge toward the bottom, Thomson considered his options. There remained only one possible way the *Pisces* was going to return to the surface: releasing an untested 407-pound (185 kg) drop weight would have to compensate for whatever buoyancy had been lost in the explosion. But had the drop-weight mechanism been damaged in the blast? An emergency drop weight is exactly what it sounds like; a weight that can be dropped from the sub if a large and sudden increase in buoyancy is needed. On the *Pisces*, the weight was held to the frame by a long, finely threaded crank. Thomson's struggle to release the weight was recorded on tape.

BOEING ENGINEER WARREN JOSLYN, ABOARD THE *HUDSON EXPLORER*, STUDIES INFORMATION RELAYED BY THE DESCENDING *PISCES*.

"Fourteen hundred feet and still descending. (Creak, creak, pant, puff, puff.) Fifteen hundred feet and still descending. (Puff, puff, puff.) Sixteen hundred feet and still descending."

Finally, the weight fell away.

"Thank Christ," said Thomson, to no one. "It's gone."

At this point the *Pisces* should have shot up like a bubble. It did not. It merely slowed in its descent. What Thomson had failed to take into account was Archimedes' principle; an engineer had suggested a drop weight of 407 pounds (185 kg) in water. Thomson had made the weight 407 pounds (185 kg) on land. Still the *Pisces* continued to sink, though Thomson, with desperate optimism, thought it might be descending more slowly. Down, down it drifted for another 100 feet (30 m), where it came to a standstill, suspended in the black waters. Thomson studied the depth gauge. Nineteen hundred and seventy feet (600 m). The *Pisces* had reached the test depth. But would it rise? The *Pisces'* searchlight sent a core into the dark water, but there was nothing to indicate whether the craft was going to hold steady or ascend. Thomson shivered in the chill cabin. The hull ticked under the tremendous pressure.

Again Thomson peered at the depth gauge and considered his immediate future. The *Pisces*, designed to take two and even three passengers on day-long expeditions, had enough oxygen to last for forty-eight hours. If Thomson shut down all systems and tried to conserve air, he might last for sixty hours. After that, he knew, would come shortness of breath and blackout. While considering his fate, he kept his eyes on the depth gauge. Slowly, like a minute hand on a clock, the gauge indicated the sub was rising. Thomson could only watch the controls and hope there would be no more catastrophes.

Far above on the surface, daylight was dwindling. The US Navy vessel had discreetly concluded its tests and steamed away, leaving the *Hudson Explorer* alone in the inlet. It had been hours since last contact with the *Pisces*. With night falling, the crew realized there soon wouldn't be enough light to take bearings. They would be unable to hold the *Explorer* over the spot where the *Pisces* had descended. Trice ran the boat to the nearby shore, where the scow was secured, and started the power plant to provide light for a reference point. Then all they could do was return to the approximate place where the *Pisces* had gone down and wait helplessly for the sub to reappear. Other than to refill a cup of coffee or search for yet another pack of cigarettes, no one could move. The group huddled on deck, scanning the waters for any sign of the *Pisces*. If it did surface, it was important they spot it quickly. The *Pisces* rode so low in the water that, between evening winds and tidal currents, it could easily drift away, unnoticed, for miles. The US submersible *Ben Franklin* had drifted for six hours on the surface before her support ship located her. Another, named the *Alvin*, had been lost for ten hours off Bermuda.

They need not have worried. From the black waters came a light that some of the crew later described as an atomic bomb going off. Others felt a near-religious experience. It was the *Pisces* ascending, led by its powerful headlights. The submersible bobbed to the surface. It was midnight. Thomson had been down for eight hours.

What had caused the *Pisces* to sink was an explosion—actually an implosion of one of the two smaller 16-inch spheres used for ballast and trim control. The electrical cable from the transducer (hydrophone) was cut off at the same time and that ended any communication on the underwater telephone. Thomson had been lucky. If even one more of the spheres had gone, releasing the drop weight might well have been futile. But he was jubilant. The ballast sphere was a simple thing to replace, and the *Pisces*, as far as the military needed to know, was good to 1,970 feet (600 m).

Although they had no way of knowing it at the time, the *Pisces'* inventors had launched a technological renaissance in BC. The success of the little submersible on the torpedo range, and in subsequent salvage operations, led to the building of more *Pisces* crafts—ten in all. International corporations—including some who had entertained the "T-shirt boys" yet failed to complete their own subs—noted the upstarts, and within a few years versions of the *Pisces* were working on cable-laying projects in the Atlantic and capping oil wells in the North Sea. Experts from all over the world

WAITING, WAITING, WAITING.
DON SORTE AND AL TRICE
HOPE FOR WORD FROM THE
SUBMERGED *PISCES*.

came to visit, including scientists from the USSR, one of whom went on to lead an underwater exploration of the *Titanic*. As HYCo grew, so did the support industries around it—a plethora of Lower Mainland firms specializing in underwater communication, propulsion, navigation and remote-control vehicles.

Unfortunately the financial side of HYCo never proved as buoyant as their submersibles. Some of this was the fault of the owners, who insisted on redesigning the sub every time they received an order. Some was the fault of the Trudeau government, who, when HYCo signed a crucial multimillion-dollar deal to sell subs to the USSR, gave in to US pressure and revoked the company's export permit. After fifteen years, in 1979, HYCo folded as a business, though its subs, in the hands of other firms, continue to work to this day, as do its former employees, many of whom manage Vancouver's elite underwater research firms. Among this crowd, HYCo is referred to as the "kindergarten"—the place where it all began.

The only HYCo sub that didn't endure was the first. The *Pisces I* became—via a complex business deal—the property of Vickers Oceanics. Vickers transported it to England, then had the sub dismantled. In the chaos of nationalization in the 1970s the firm somehow lost the parts. Its skookum frame and now-prehistoric electronics may still be lurking in the corner of a Midlands warehouse. Or they may be part of a 1998 Jaguar hurtling along the freeway. No one knows.

But back on the wooden scow that December night in 1966, all that mattered to Trice, Sorte and Thomson was that their idea had worked. As they toasted glasses of champagne, jokes were swapped about how those aboard the *Hudson Explorer* had debated pouring the bottles into the water as a memorial to Thomson. They secured the *Pisces* and made ready for the long, slow haul back to Vancouver. For their success they had only themselves to thank. And a US torpedo with lousy ears.

(TOP) MACK THOMSON EMERGES TRIUMPHANTLY FROM THE SUBMERSIBLE.

(BOTTOM) THE HYCO CREW CELEBRATE THE RETURN OF THE *PISCES* WITH CHAMPAGNE. LEFT TO RIGHT: DON SORTE, MACK THOMSON, SOMETIME BOUNCER PETEY EDGAR, AL TRICE.

Lootaas

n October 1989, a Haida dugout arrived at a wharf below city hall in Paris, France. Forty-eight feet long and freighted with twenty paddlers and passengers, including its builder, the enigmatic Native artist Bill Reid, the *Lootaas* had been paddled and towed 80 nautical miles up the Seine River from Rouen. As it docked the crew scrambled onto the shore, chanting tribal songs and drumming. Some were clad in deerskins, others were streaked with paint. All looked mighty. Delete the winking video cameras and the background rumble of the city, and passersby could be forgiven for thinking they were watching a seventeenth-century war party preparing for battle.

MOMENTS AFTER IT WAS LAUNCHED, THE *LOOTAAS* IS PADDLED FROM THE BEACH AT SKIDEGATE.

A CENTURY BEFORE THE *LOOTAAS*, THE SHORELINE AT SKIDEGATE WAS CROWDED WITH CANOES.

And, in some ways, they would be right; the *Lootaas*'s arrival in Paris was an invasion of sorts. The groundwork for the insurgency had been set two years earlier when the vast Musée de l'Homme in Paris placed an innocent call to Reid in Vancouver. The museum announced that, as part of an upcoming celebration honouring French anthropologist Claude Levi-Strauss, it intended to display some of Reid's jewellery, masks and carvings. Reid was rightly pleased; the museum had never before featured work by a living artist. Yet he deigned to make a further suggestion: why not also showcase what he thought was one of his most important works, the *Lootaas*, the dugout canoe he had made for Vancouver's Expo 86? They jumped. Then Reid set the hook. "I told them they could have the boat as long as they

took the paddlers," he later explained, a coy smile curling at his large-featured face.

(Launched as *Lootaas*, or "Wave Eater," the dugout later had its name changed when a Haida orthographer pointed out that *Lootaas* actually translated as "Sand Eater." The craft is now known, more correctly, as *Lootaa* or *Luu Taa*. But because Reid knew it as *Lootaas*, this text maintains the original spelling.)

The journey became a showcase for the Haida Nation. Claiming that Canada had no legal or moral authority over them because the Haida had never been conquered, the paddlers refused to use Canadian passports and travelled to France on a diplomatic "safe passage" arrangement designed to shorten the usual requirements for entering the country. On the Seine, Haida escorting the paddlers on two barges ripped Canadian flags, thoughtfully provided by the embassy. Though French villagers were visibly perplexed that the *Lootaas*'s hefty crew did not conform to their headdress-and-redskin image of Natives, the Haida did not change their approach. Wrist watches and big runners mixed with robes and ritual. The museum wanted them to paddle all the way, but the Haida hadn't counted on pollution so bad it made them retch. After two days on the scum-laden river, the exhausted crew hitched a ride on an accompanying barge. Hollywood Indians might paddle upstream twenty hours a day, but real Indians—like the Haida—did as they pleased.

If the *Lootaas*'s journey disappointed the French, it did not show in Paris. After the ceremonial dance the crew was greeted by a troup of dignitaries, including Paris mayor Jaques Chirac, and the aging Levi-Strauss, who praised Reid for his leadership role in the resurrection of Native art. Then the *Lootaas* was hoisted from the water, cleaned, and readied as a centrepiece of the exhibition. It was a great moment for Reid, and also for the Haida culture that inspired him.

If, as Bill Reid claimed, the true power in Northwest art "is the movement by which it got to be that shape," then the *Lootaas*'s inspiration can be found in a voyage taken

THE GREAT *LOOTAAS* FLOATS
HIGH IN THE WATER AT ITS
LAUNCHING.

by a pretty, long-haired Native girl at the turn of the century. The girl's name was Sophie Gladstone; she would become Reid's mother. The voyage was from the settlement of Skidegate, near her birth village of Tanu in the Queen Charlotte Islands, to an Anglican residential school near Chilliwack. The reason: her parents, distrustful of the old ways, believed she would be best off away from the islands and educated.

At school, Sophie's memory was cleansed. Knowledge of the Raven and Eagle clans, of mythological Chief Githawn (or "Salmon Eater") who led six canoe-loads of seagoers from the foam to create the Haida, were banished in favour of the English arts of elocution, presentation, comportment. She learned to sew, set a table. Sophie graduated a model of middle-class manners. In modern vernacular she was an "apple," red on the outside, white on the inside.

After graduation Sophie formalized her immersion into white culture by marrying an American hotelkeeper of Scots–German descent. William Reid was a blustery, end-of-the-rails man who chased boomtowns across the Northwest. Sophie took his surname, set up a starchy-doily-and-scones household and bore her first child, Bill Reid.

In many ways, Reid's life can be seen as the equal and opposite of his mother's: she left her Haida origins for the white middle-class realm; Bill Reid made the return trip. Raised in a world of short pants and lemonade, Reid's understanding of Native culture did not extend beyond the bracelets on his mother's arm. His first significant contact with Haida life was when he was twenty-two. He spent a week perched on a clapboard porch in Skidegate, watching his maternal grandfather, Charles Gladstone, carving. Charles had apprenticed with Chief Charles Edenshaw, the last of the great nineteenth century Haida carvers. He couldn't speak English; Bill couldn't speak Haida. Somehow, though, a spore was set. Life and living kept him from pursuing his dreams until a happenstance bit of luck set him into jewellery-making. He abandoned a career as a CBC news announcer, and turned to art.

Like a hard-pan farmer let loose on river-bottom tilth, Reid worked Native forms with a passion. It was his white upbringing, he said, that made him appreciate Native art so much. Incorporating European-style craftsmanship with a classic Northwest aesthetic, his works were first good, then great. In the 1960s and 1970s he made jewellery, prints and, most famously, he sculpted. His celebrated *Raven and the First Men*, depicting a Haida genesis, brought a new freshness and originality to traditional Native art forms. By the 1980s, Reid's works were fetching five-figure bids at Sotheby's international auctions. Critics called him one of Canada's best artists.

In the early 1980s Reid received an invitation to carve a dugout canoe for Expo. The *Lootaas* was to be part of a massive celebration of Native culture, and it fitted with the fair's transportation theme. Though Reid had developed Parkinson's disease, a muscular affliction that left him weak and shaky, he accepted. There was, he hoped, a chance that the dugout could jump-start a resurgence in Native carving in the Charlottes. He had tried once before, when he carved a totem pole on the beach at Skidegate in 1978, but he later thought the pole too static to be of but short-term interest. A dugout, with its ongoing use, might have a more lasting effect.

The dugout project also attracted Reid because it suggested a path to finish the journey to his Native roots. From working on several small dugouts, he had sensed that the canoe itself was the template for the essential forms of Native art. "Inevitably," he theorized, "people who spent as much time as the Haida spent working on canoes would take the lines that were familiar to them when they moved to other creative activity." The canoe may thus have influenced the representational designs found throughout Native art: ovoid, U-form and formline, the widening and narrowing tapering line that is the basis of Native design. (Reid's interest in dugouts would continue through to his most famous work, *The Spirit of Haida Gwaii* or *The Black Canoe*, which features a dugout overflowing with the creatures of Haida mythology and stands outside the Canadian embassy in Washington, DC. Another version, *The Jade Canoe*, dominates the new departure hall at the Vancouver International Airport.)

All this was going to stay so much theory, however, unless a big cedar could be located. If the dugout was going to be as massive as planned, a log 6 feet (2 m) through had to be found. The area around Skidegate was mostly a mange of second growth. Forests on much of the rest of the islands were under tenure to MacMillan Bloedel, whom Reid described as "difficult squatters" on Native land. Reid and a cooperative MB manager did search out a single huge western red cedar not far from Skidegate, but it was discovered to be cracked and knotted. Eventually another specimen was located and, with help from a fleet of corporate heavy equipment, was bulled 25 miles (40 km) to a carving shed at Skidegate.

There was a time when finding a log would not have been such a task. From the

THE CANOE MAKER'S TOOLS ARE AS SIMPLE AND ELEGANT AS THE CRAFT THEY CREATE.

giant cedars that grew on the rain-drenched islands, pre-twentieth-century Natives selected trees that were close to a village or navigable stream. They felled them with controlled burns, then hollowed them with stone or iron adzes. The process sounds laborious, but a European observer in the 1800s noted that two journeymen could make a 20-foot dugout in less than three weeks. Compared to the amount of time it takes to pay off an automobile—the modern equivalent of the dugout—the ancient boat-builders made good time.

Easy access to material combined with the luxury of living in a food-rich environment meant Native people could have all the dugouts they wanted. They carved versatile versions for fishing and berry gathering, tiny craft for kids and great high-prowed dugouts for war. There were even showboat vessels, built for nothing more than ostentation. One of these, the "Chief" dugout at Masset, was said to be 90 feet long. Another "vanity" dugout was made at Nitinat. Fifty-five feet long and 6 feet deep, it was too big to safely navigate the tidal rips and currents, and was abandoned in the bush.

There were so many dugouts, they plugged village beaches like vehicles plug urban highways. At Skidegate, an abundance of canoes made it difficult for visitors to find a place to park. A Hudson's Bay Company trader at a supposedly remote mainland outpost reported seeing eight hundred dugouts pass per month. When Thomas Barnett, a contemporary of George Vancouver, arrived in the *Gustavus III* off Langara Island at the northwest corner of the Queen Charlottes, six hundred Haida dugouts encircled his ship. It has been estimated that at the time of the *Discovery*'s survey there were enough dugouts on the coast to put the entire population afloat, plus many of its material goods, too.

Two healthy men in a canoe could travel 35 nautical miles per day, a distance that would take them, for example, from Skidegate far past Tlell on the east coast of Graham Island, or from the mouth of the Fraser River across the Strait of Georgia to Nanaimo. In the days before sea otter hunting, when sea otters kept the kelp-eating sea urchin population in check, great banks of kelp lined the coast, creating a sheltered highway that broke the West Coast surf. For centuries the Haida and other Native nations used this route, or else boldly set out across open waters in their seaworthy craft to trade, make war, make peace or explore. Dugouts were important

THE *LOOTAAS* WAS BUILT ONLY AFTER MUCH TESTING BY BILL REID AND OTHER CARVERS. HERE REID WORKS ON A SMALL DUGOUT, TAKING LINES FROM A MODEL CANOE IN THE FOREGROUND.

"tools of empire," just as steamers like the *Beaver* were to England and other European powers.

For the Haida, especially, living in a land only accessible by water, it was horrifyingly inevitable that the dugout—the craft that brought Chief Githawn to the land—was literally the vessel of their demise. In the mid-1800s, a party of Haida paddled south to trade at the new HBC fort in Victoria. They returned with blankets infected with smallpox. In one year their population plummeted from ten thousand to one thousand. The culture was decimated, and young Haida, like Sophie Gladstone, turned to the new white culture.

Bill Reid learned that it wasn't only the big cedars that were gone from the islands. A lot of ancient wisdom and lore had vanished, too. It had been seventy years since a large dugout was carved in Skidegate. Most old carvers were dead, and those who did remember the grand days, when dozens of 50- and 60-foot canoes were pulled up on the village's beach, were vague on specifics. Some people thought Reid should trust his instincts, but he was too much the jeweller to subject a priceless 750-year-old piece of wood to the blows of an ungoverned adze. If anything, the realization he might not have time to carve another canoe if this one failed made him even more methodical. He eventually found what he was looking for in archives and museum collections, though he also discovered some alarming errors. One anthropologist recommended steaming a dugout for two days—a recipe for overcooking similar to boiling rice for a week. And in the American Museum of Natural History's prized Native collection, Reid found a Haida dugout built backward—with the bow made from the butt of the tree.

Though armed with a PhD's worth of material, Reid still didn't feel ready to set into the log. First, he announced to the team of carvers working on the project that they were going to build a fibreglass model. They did, and it served as a prototype for the cedar dugout. Meanwhile, carver Stacey "Jags" Brown, Reid's son-in-law, was experimenting with steaming. He carved a tiny dugout and steamed it in his wife's roasting pot on the kitchen stove. From the fibreglass model they took patterns and laid them onto the log. The delays caused the head carver to walk away, but Reid was steadfast. "He thought I was taking too many calculations," Reid explained to a visiting journalist, one of many who visited the specially erected carving shed at Skidegate. "He believed in racial memory and all that stuff, and letting your instincts decide how you carve. I say you get the same result with good pencil work."

The explanation was classic Reid—honest and straightforward. But it also goes a way to explaining the tension that infused the project, too. As if his fellow carvers never read newspapers or listened to the newscasts, Reid frequently let fly with some stunningly candid remarks:

On Haida history: "They know they were self-sufficient, and they believe they were great warriors. In fact, they were raiders, not warriors. They did not believe battles were a good thing. They believed that sneaking up to someone and hitting them over the head was a good thing. They were pretty regularly beaten up by the Kwakiutl."

On the Haida's touted longhouse in Skidegate, hailed as evidence of cultural resurgence: "[It was] completely the creation of outsiders. What the band wanted was two mobile homes shoved together—an instant office."

On Native modern art: "I never believed in this so-called renaissance of Northwest Coast Indian culture, nor that I had any great contribution to make to the art form. I did what I did because I enjoyed doing it."

The actual carving, the slow chop and hack, the measuring and remeasuring, took three months. The brunt of the work was done by Haida carvers, working on the honey-coloured red cedar under wide skylights. Piecemeal, they reduced the great log to a thickness of 2 inches (5 cm) on the bottom and a mere seven-eighths of an inch (2.2 cm) on the sides.

Reid helped sporadically. Tired and irritable, he often slumped in a chair against the wall of the carving shed. When he wanted to rise he hoisted an arm, as if seeking a handshake. That was the signal for a friend to hoist him to his feet. Then he shuffled to the shaping log. Only when he picked up a tool or a pencil did his hands stop the interminable, mind-of-their-own shaking.

Though Reid and the carvers often talked of "finding" the dugout in the wood, of working with the wood instead of imposing a preconceived shape on it, they knew everything ultimately depended on the steaming of the wooden shell. Steaming is the

THE FIBREGLASS *LOO PLEX* SERVED AS A FULL-SIZED MODEL FOR THE *LOOTAAS*.

transformative event in a dugout's genesis, altering it from a brittle, unseaworthy shell to a strong, lithe craft. The straight sides expand out to give the canoe the fluted form, and the bow and stern curl up. Steaming can also cause a canoe to crack in half. Reid called it "a co-operative and sometimes antagonistic relationship between boat and builder."

He might have added antagonism between boatbuilder and the Gods of machinery. On the long-awaited February morning that the dugout was to be steamed, the well at Skidegate sucked air. Seawater wouldn't do. While Reid measured and remeasured the hull (temporarily dubbed Murphy, in honour of the well-known law), someone ran to fetch the village firetruck. The truck's pipe was fed, umbilically, into a drum, where the water was heated. When the water was hot, it was piped into the hull, which had been lined with chicken wire and wood chips (in the old days it was branches and kelp). Hot rocks were wheelbarrowed up a ramp and tipped into the dugout. Then the craft was covered with a tarpaulin and, like a pot of tea, left to steep.

Several hours later, stones and water still hissed at the bottom of the craft. The carvers placed their hands on the warm hull, feeling for movement. The outside was warm but hard; inside, the cedar fibres had become malleable. One Haida man jammed his arm under the tarp to the elbow. "It feels like..." Then he said something that made the other men snicker.

Before steaming, the hull was 52 inches (132 cm) at its widest point. It quickly gained 6 inches (15 cm), then fifty minutes after the last hot rocks were added, it registered another 4 inches (10 cm). Thwarts were inserted to keep the hull spread wide. The bow and stern rose, leaving the carefully designed keel flat.

It was a tense time for everyone. Unnoticed, a rock could roll from the bed of

(TOP AND BOTTOM) STEAMING IS THE CRUCIAL STAGE IN THE CONSTRUCTION OF ANY CEDAR CANOE, LARGE OR SMALL.

chips and scorch a hole in the hull. A quirk in the wood could cause it to contort unevenly, leaving one side more swollen than the other. Worse still, the spirits could have taken offence to a broken taboo, a carver who did not remain celibate, a thoughtless observer who stood at the end of the canoe when the water was poured in, and the whole thing would fall apart.

Nothing disastrous happened, but the hull's expansion stopped despite steady tapping on the thwarts. Reid wanted the canoe to be wider. He summoned several dozen bystanders. They lined up on each side, hands on the gunwales. On a command from Reid they heaved. Like prying open the mouth of a massive animal, they pulled out the sides another 10 inches (25 cm), then held them there. Reid, hair askew, deftly sawed a piece of wood to a hollered length and jammed it into the stretched hull. The team, puffing and red, moved down the hull and repeated the task.

It had been dark for two hours when Reid announced that the canoe was complete. The hull still needed to be sanded and varnished and seats had to be built but, in its essential form, it was now a canoe. That morning it had been a carved log. The carvers and crowd cele-

WORKERS INSERT THWARTS INTO THE HULL, RECENTLY STEAMED AND STILL MALLEABLE.

brated with drumming, singing, applause.

Later, with the fecund smell of wet cedar still filling the air, the villagers trundled out. The new dugout sat in the middle of the shed; the old carver was slumped in a seat against a wall. "In case of serious accident," said a nearby sign, "don't bleed on the finished part." Reid raised his hand in the hope that someone would shake it, but the gesture was misinterpreted and he was helped to his feet.

An axe lay against a block. Reid clasped it in his suddenly sure hands and deftly split the block in two. Clutching one half to his chest he scratched several words, repaired a mistake, scratched some more. A passing tug growled in the nearby inlet. Reid hobbled to a window and propped his sign on a shelf. "Joy," it read, "is a well made object."

Bill Reid died in March 1998. In early July, a carved bentwood box containing his ashes was placed in the bow of the Lootaas *and the dugout paddled from Skidegate, where it is now stored in the longhouse beside the museum, to his mother's birthplace, the abandoned coastal village of Tanu. Following a simple, elegant ceremony amid the forest-scented surroundings, the artist's ashes were scattered over ground that was once home to his ancient ancestors. The* Lootaas, *a true westcoaster and a reincarnation of the craft that had defined coastal transportation before the coming of Europeans, had brought Reid home.*

Selected Bibliography

Books

Anderson, Bern. *Surveyor of the Sea: The Life and Voyages of Capt. George Vancouver.* Toronto: University of Toronto Press, 1960.

Anderson, Doris. *The Columbia is Coming!* Sidney BC: Gray's Publishing, 1982.

Assu, Harry, with Inglis, Joy. *Assu of Cape Mudge: Recollections of a Coastal Indian Chief.* Vancouver: University of BC Press, 1989.

Audain, James. *Alex Dunsmuir's Dilemma.* Victoria: Sunnylane Publishing, 1964.

Barman, Jean. *The West Beyond the West: A History of British Columbia.* Toronto: University of Toronto Press, 1996.

Canadian Hydrographic Service. *British Columbia Pilot*, vol. I. Ottawa: Marine Services Branch, Department of Mines and Technical Surveys, 1965.

_____. *British Columbia Pilot*, vol. II. Ottawa: Marine Services Branch, Department of Energy, Mines and Resources, 1969.

Carrington, Philip. *The Anglican Church in Canada.* Toronto: Collins, 1963.

Cherrington, John A. *The Fraser Valley.* Madeira Park BC: Harbour Publishing, 1992.

Cox, Mary Aline. *Saga of a Seafarer: The Annals of Capt. William Irving.* New Westminster BC: Columbia Company, 1966.

Craven, Margaret. *I Heard the Owl Call My Name.* Toronto: Clarke, Irwin, 1967.

Crosse, John. Thermopylae *and the Age of the Clippers*, 2nd ed. Vancouver: Historia Publishers, 1970.

Downs, Art. *British Columbia-Yukon Sternwheeler Days* Surrey BC: Heritage House, n.d.

Drushka, Ken. *Against Wind and Weather: The History of Towboating in British Columbia.* Vancouver: Douglas & McIntyre, 1991.

Fisher, Robin. *Contact and Conflict: Indian–European Relations in British Columbia, 1774–1890*, 2nd ed. Vancouver: University of BC Press, 1992.

_____. *Vancouver's Voyage: Charting the Northwest Coast, 1791–1795.* Vancouver: Douglas & McIntyre, 1992.

Gibson, Gordon. *Bull of the Woods: The Gordon Gibson Story.* Vancouver: Douglas & McIntyre, 1980.

Greene, Ruth. *Personality Ships of BC.* West Vancouver: Marine Tapestry Publications, 1969.

Hacking, R. Norman and Lamb, W. Kaye. *The Princess Story: A Century and a Half of West Coast Shipping.* Vancouver: Mitchell Press, 1974.

_____. *Captain William Moore: B.C.'s Amazing Frontiersman.* Surrey BC: Heritage House, 1993.

Haig-Brown, Alan. *Fishing For a Living.* Madeira Park BC: Harbour Publishing, 1993.

Haig-Brown, Alan and Blacklaws, Rick. *The Fraser River.* Madeira Park BC: Harbour Publishing, 1996.

Helgesen, Marion I. *Footprints: Pioneer Families of the Metchosin District, Southern Vancouver Island, 1851–1900.* Metchosin: Metchosin School Museum Society, 1983.

Henry, Tom. *The Good Company: An Affectionate History of the Union Steamships.* Madeira Park BC: Harbour Publishing, 1994.

Johnson, R. Byron. *Very Far West Indeed: A Few Rough Experiences on the North-West Pacific Coast.* London: Sampson Low, Marston, Low, & Searle, 1872.

Jupp, Ursula. *Home Port: Victoria.* Victoria: Morriss Printing, 1985.

Kemp, Peter, ed. *The Oxford Companion to Ships and the Sea.* Oxford: Oxford University Press, 1993.

Lamb, W. Kaye, ed. *A Voyage of Discovery to the North Pacific Ocean and Round the World, 1791–1795.* London: The

Hakluyt Society, 1984.

Lillard, Charles. *Seven Shillings a Year: The History of Vancouver Island*. Ganges BC: Horsdal & Schubart, 1993.

London, Jack. *The Sea Wolf*. Pleasantville NY: Reader's Digest Association, 1989.

Lubbock, Basil. *The China Clippers*. Glasgow: Brown, Son and Ferguson, 1984.

McCann, Leonard G. *The Honourable Company's* Beaver. Vancouver: Vancouver Museums and Planetarium Association, 1980.

MacGregor, David. *Fast Sailing Ships: Their Design and Construction 1775–1875*. Annapolis MD: Naval Institute Press, 1973.

Matheson, Marny. *Clippers for the Record*. Melbourne: Spectrum Publications, 1984.

Miles, Fraser. *Slow Boat on Rum Row*. Madeira Park BC: Harbour Publishing, 1992.

Morton, Harry. *The Wind Commands: Sailors & Sailing Ships in the Pacific*. Vancouver: University of BC Press, 1975.

Murray, Peter. *The Vagabond Fleet: a Chronicle of the North Pacific Sealing Schooner Trade*. Victoria: Sono Nis Press, 1988.

Neel, David. *The Great Canoes: Reviving a Northwest Coast Tradition*. Vancouver: Douglas & McIntyre, 1995.

Newell, Gordon. *Pacific Tugboats*. Seattle: Superior Publishing, 1957.

Parker, Marion and Tyrell, Robert. *Rumrunner: The Life and Times of Johnny Schnarr*. Victoria: Orca Book Publishers, 1988.

Rushton, Gerald A. *Whistle Up the Inlet: The Union Steamship Story*. Vancouver: J.J. Douglas, 1974.

Sager, Eric. *Ships and Memories: Merchant Seafarers in Canada's Age of Steam*. Vancouver: University of BC Press, 1993.

Shackleton, Philip and Roberts, Kenneth G. *The Canoe: A history of the craft from Panama to the Arctic*. Toronto: Macmillan of Canada, 1983.

Shadbolt, Doris. *Bill Reid*. Vancouver: Douglas & McIntyre, 1988.

Ward, W. Peter and McDonald, Robert A.J. *British Columbia: Historical Readings*. Vancouver: Douglas & McIntyre, 1981.

White, Howard, ed. *Raincoast Chronicles*, Nos. 1–17, Madeira Park BC: BC Coast Historical Society.

Journals

BC Studies

The Beaver

British Columbia Historical Quarterly

Equinox

The Fisherman

Harbour & Shipping

Maclean's

Oregon Historical Quarterly

Resolution

West Coast Mariner

West Coast Fisherman

Acknowledgements

Many people contributed to this book: historians, journalists, old-timers, sailors, archivists, editors, photographers, friends, family. The principal written sources are listed in the Selected Bibliography, and I am indebted to these book and periodical writers, whose material was particularly useful: J.E. Roberts, Hugh Garling, John Crosse, Ken Drushka, Alan Haig-Brown, Micheal Hatley, Stephen Godfrey, David R. Conn, Gerald Rushton, Ruth Greene and Merilyn Mohr.

The task of archival work was made easier by all the staff of the BC Archives and Records Services; the Vancouver Maritime Museum, especially Rachel Grant, Leonard McCann and James P. Delgado; and the Maritime Museum of BC, particularly Lynn Reid and Angela Mitonni.

The chapter on *Pisces I* is largely based on interviews with Al Trice and an unpublished manuscript by Ken Dinsley.

I am also grateful for information supplied by Andy Wilson, Lorne Christensen, Doug Hartley, Richard Hebda, David Francis, Ole Chickite, researcher Caroline Rueckert and (though they did not always know they were being interviewed) towboaters Barry Fairall and Bruce Davidson.

Any errors are my responsibility.

Photograph and Illustration Credits

Anglican Provincial Synod of BC Archives, Vancouver: pages 86 (PSA5-1003), 88 (PSA5-844), 89 (top: PSA5-846, bottom: PSA5-1105), 90 (PSA5-850).

L.D. Belveal collection: page 53.

Rolf Bettner: pages 175, 177, 180.

British Columbia Archives and Records Service: pages 10 (PDP02252), 13 (A01932), 19 (PDP05374), 20 (PDP00445), 21 (PDP00206), 26 (2016), 27 (A00010), 29 (A1228), 30 (A0009), 32 (A07731), 36 (PDP02687), 40 (A06750), 42 (A03579), 43 (G02681), 47 (10422), 48 (left: PDP02234, right: B02273), 56 (B07530), 61 (G04856), 66 (G04857), 67 (A04694), 75 (D05993), 78 (B00617), 79 (top: F05169, bottom: B00619), 80 (F03426), 84-85 (B05475), 92 (E07877), 95 (E1654), 98 (F08204), 99 (D06890), 100 (D04329), 103 (C04900), 104 (bottom: B02263), 105 (E04042), 108-9 (D01777), 124 (D05825), 174 (B03660).

Ole Chickite collection: page 139.

Lorne Christensen collection: page 49.

Jane Elworthy collection: page 142.

D. Hartley collection: pages 72-73, 74, 82, 83.

Langley Centennial Museum: page 24.

Carey Linde: page 176.

Maritime Museum of British Columbia, Victoria, BC: pages 22-23, 34-35, 51, 60, 65, 70, 77, 104 (top and middle), 123 (bottom), 140-41, 143.

Robert McVittie: front cover, pages 8-9.

Pete Van de Putte: page 148.

Seaspan collection: pages 144, 147, 150.

Al Trice collection: pages 152-53, 156, 160, 162, 163, 164, 165, 166, 167, 169, 170, 171 (top and bottom).

University of British Columbia Library, Special Collections: page 15.

University of British Columbia, Museum of Anthropology, Bill McLennan: pages 178, 181 (top and bottom), 182.

University of British Columbia, Museum of Anthropology, J.L. Gijssen: pages 172-73, 183.

City of Vancouver Archives: pages 87, 120-21, 122.

Vancouver Maritime Museum: pages 11, 16, 18, 27, 31, 37, 39, 41, 44-45, 46, 52, 54, 55, 57 (top and bottom), 58-59, 62 (top), 63, 64, 69, 71, 81, 91, 96-97, 101, 106, 107, 110, 111 (top and bottom), 113, 114, 115, 117 (top and bottom), 118, 123 (top), 125, 126, 128, 129, 131, 132-33, 135, 138, 139, 151.

Vancouver Public Library: pages 28 (800), 33 (798).

Index